Beyond Resistance

The Institutional Church Meets the Postmodern World

Beyond Resistance

The Institutional Church
Meets the Postmodern World

John Dorhauer

Exploration Press
Chicago, Illinois

Exploration Press
Chicago Theological Seminary
1407 E. 60th Street
Chicago, Illinois 60637

ISBN: 978-0913552-74-2

Library of Congress Control Number: 2015944682

CONTENTS

CHAPTER ONE

Death with Dignity

"I'm not afraid of death. I just don't want to be there when it happens."

- Woody Allen

Let's be honest... churches are dying.

Well, some of them are. Many more are going to. The combination of membership losses, the rising costs of maintaining budgetary expenses that include full-time clergy, large pieces of aging property, and a steep decline in the economy have placed many of our churches in very precarious times.

I want to examine some of the causes of this diminishment in vitality and talk about some of the responses to it that church leaders should be considering.

David Greenhaw, president of Eden Seminary, spoke two years ago at a Phoenix area church. He reported that for every year of this country's life, the Church in America grew a minimum of 1% a year, without exception, until 1961. Since that time, and again without exception, the Church has declined in membership a minimum of 1 percent a year.

Fundamentalists have argued that the Church has become too liberal. It is an apostate Church. God has condemned this Church to inevitable decline because of its unwillingness to follow scripture to the letter of the law. This argument lost steam when, in the last decade, many of the large, fundamentalist mega-churches started bleeding members and it began to dawn on everyone that significant membership losses happened without regard to theological orientation. The truth about these losses is far more complex.

It is not the purpose of this book to write about the causes of this decline, nor about the inevitability that some churches won't survive. I feel it is still important that I mention three things that are having a deep impact on church decline: birthrates, the cost of maintaining aging property, and postmodernity have all significantly changed the landscape of the Church.

I am being a bit selective here. Others will look to different causes, and they would be right to do so. Again, what we are experiencing

7

in the Church today is the result of a complex array of issues that defies simple explanation. What I offer here is admittedly biased and incomplete.

Birthrate

An often-overlooked factor is perhaps the simplest one of all: birthrates. Let's look at some numbers.

In 1910, the birth rate (the number of live births per thousand in population) in the United States was 30.1. In 2010, it was 13.4. Over the last 100 years, the birth rate has dropped almost a full twenty per thousand. There was not a decade in those 100 years when the birthrate did not drop. In June of 2013, the *Washington Times* reported that the fertility rate (the number of children per woman) in America dropped to 1.89%, well below the replacement level of 2.1% (the rate at which our current population base can sustain or replace itself).

We can talk about the shift in America from an agrarian to an urban culture; the shift from the Industrial Revolution to the Information Age; the sexual revolution; pharmaceuticals that help women control unwanted pregnancies; better sex education; and even the impact of climate control on population rate. All are critical factors that affect how the culture in general, and how individual women in particular, approach decisions about childbirth.

We cannot, however, escape the simple fact that America, for a long time, was building more and more churches to sustain an ever-growing population. We built them because we needed them.

Most churches hit their peak in membership sometime in the two decades following the Second World War. We call the children of those war brides the Baby Boomer generation. Because of those large families, church membership grew. And, as white flight led to an abandonment of the city and middle-class families moved to the suburbs, more and more new churches were required to meet the needs of shifting populations. Many of those churches even built day schools so that working families had somewhere safe to take their children during the week.

It should come as no surprise that this final year of boomer births would also be the last year that American churchgoers saw their membership numbers grow.

There can be little doubt that we don't need as many churches today. Supply has outstripped demand. It is inevitable that some of our churches are going to close. I listen to pastors from previous generations describe an "If you build it, they will come" phenomenon. Those days are gone.

I don't want to imply that it is as simple as this, but we have to consider whether some of the churches that were built to sustain the population base that grew in the aftermath of WWII are simply no longer viable due to a steep decline in birthrates.

For at least the last twenty years, church growth has not been about meeting the demands of a growing population—and certainly not about creating more and more space for all those new believers who are demanding that we build more churches to meet their ever-growing needs. Denominations are finding that those old methods no longer work.

Property

Closely related to birthrate is the cost of maintaining aging properties, especially when many of the buildings erected to house worshippers sit largely empty most Sundays.

It is assumed that to be a church you have to have your own property. This makes sense. I don't want to create the impression that by naming property as a contributing cause of decline, I am saying that a church should not own property. What I do mean to suggest is that property must serve a missional purpose. Too many churches hold on to buildings long after there is no identifiable mission. There can be no doubt that once this happens, the amount of resources needed to maintain them becomes a serious drain on missional resources. Few churches that I know ever ask questions about the legitimacy of maintaining their property, even after their membership base has shrunk to a size no longer sufficient to justify or support it.

Churches are called into being by the Holy Spirit in order to undertake mission. Of all the work I do as an agent of the wider Church, I think the most important is reminding our church leaders that everything they do is in service to a mission.

One of my mantras is, simply, "It's about mission." Identifying that core mission and giving your heart and soul to it with passion, commitment, and excellence is a critical component to maintaining health and viability.

But as we approach what Phyllis Tickle calls "the Church's next rummage sale," we have an obligation to take a serious look at what we keep. If what we hold on to does not contribute to a mission that we know we must complete, it may be important for the sake of that mission to let it go. Staying attached to a past way of being that no longer serves a mission turns some churches into museums.

It is my experience that for many of our churches, maintaining buildings has become the mission. Long after they have lost the ability to fill to capacity the sanctuaries in which they worship, they continue to spend missional resources to maintain large, empty, unused spaces. There is a level of devotional and emotional commitment to these properties, some of which long ago stopped meeting a need.

Let there be no doubt about the beauty of these sanctuaries. Often very poor immigrants felt a duty-bound call to honor Christ by giving hard-earned and much-needed family income to the Church so that worshippers could be inspired. The buildings they left behind are testimonies to their commitment to honoring God. It wasn't just love and pride that compelled them to sacrifice so much in the effort. It was also a commitment to the gospel and a desire to leave behind a legacy that would establish the faith for many generations to come.

Let there be no doubt about their historical value. Generations of children have been baptized, confirmed, married, and buried inside these sacred walls. Pastors, often unbeknownst to them, have uttered words in sermons that changed lives forever. Town hall meetings, community rallies, protest marches, and congregational meetings have taken place in them, some of which have altered the course of history.

Let there be no doubt about the good that took place inside these buildings down through the years. Untold millions have come to the doors of these buildings knowing that they would find comfort and solace. Hard luck families needing little more than a meal or a bus ticket to the next town have knocked on doors knowing that a kind face would greet them. Men and women overcome by life's tensions and/or their choices have wandered into these sanctuaries hoping to hear a word of comfort, direction, or forgiveness.

Let there be no doubt that for many of our churches, these building still serve an important and essential mission. In some communities, groups like Alcoholics Anonymous and Parents and Friends of Lesbians And Gays discover that churches are one of the very few safe places where they can gather without fear of recrimination. Many churches are now using their vast spaces to shelter homeless families on a rotational schedule with other churches in their community. Food pantries and clothes closets are often warehoused in churches. English as a Second Language classes, after school programs, computer labs, and day care centers are found in some of our churches. There is no limit to what creative minds with a heart for mission can do with the space they control.

Having said that, it is still the case that, for many of our churches, the property has become an anchor weighing them down. Sanctuaries, classrooms, and fellowship halls sit empty through the week. The days of Sunday morning worship services filled to capacity are a part of the distant past. Upkeep on buildings must be maintained even if there is no income drawn off of it, and even if parts of the building are of no real value to the Church and its ongoing mission.

With every dollar we spend on space that serves little to no missional purpose, our collective capacity to undertake the full mission of the Church is compromised.

In May of 2010, I went to visit with one of the churches in my Conference. At their invitation, I was to spend the day with them thinking about how to renew their vitality. They were a dying church with a shrinking budget and a very small membership.

The first thing they did was hand me their budget. I noticed that they had two large expenditures, each of which took up roughly half of the budget. One was the cost of the pastor; the other was the cost of the property. The very next thing I saw was that every Sunday they collected exactly half of what they needed to sustain their budget. They were three months in arrears paying their pastor, and were trying hard to get a bank to loan them money to see them through the shortfall. No bank was willing.

After about ten minutes of quietly reading through their finances, I said to them, "This isn't rocket science, folks. You can afford your pastor or your building, but you can't have both. You have to figure out a way to be church with a pastor but not a building, or figure out how to be church with a building but not a pastor."

In January of 2012, I spent a Sunday morning in an urban church that owned almost a city block of property. About a dozen people attended worship. Worship that Sunday morning was meaningful and deeply spiritual. I was moved by the experience. I could see why those dozen or so did what they did, and why they kept coming back.

I also know they had spent the last few years agonizing over how to steward the last of their vast resources paying for their full-time pastor and their property. I met with them two nights later and told them how moved I was to be a part of their worship. I told them how important it was for them never to lose that—to hold onto that community for as long as they could.

I then told them they could continue to do that every Sunday in a room the size of the classroom we were sitting in. They didn't need that large sanctuary, much less the rest of the classrooms, offices, and other outlying buildings. I observed they were exhausting themselves by trying to figure out how to pay for all of it. I even risked sharing with them that, as a church, their mandate was mission. As a representative of the larger Church, I tried to help them see that the missional resources they were stewarding belonged not to them, but to the body of Christ. If they continued to steward those vast missional resources with no clear missional purpose, the Body of Christ as we know it was being deprived of the resources it had a right to claim for the sake of its mission.

Two other churches in the Southwest Conference voted this year to sell their buildings. They are looking for ways to live out their mission without an attachment to property. In one church, a group has split from its original congregation when it became clear to them that, if not the building itself, at the very least the location of the building (six miles outside of a small New Mexico town, a location that drew no new members there) was hindering their vision for proclaiming a gospel of extravagant welcome that they knew would help grow the Church. Citing that the Spirit was calling them to do something new, some members have begun to reshape this call to be Church without commitments to any property that they own.

These are not exceptions. These are examples of an ever-growing pool of churches whose property is seen by them to be consuming missional resources without any clear missional purpose or value; or even worse, seen as a clear hindrance to their missional purpose.

If all we do as a church is count the bodies in our sanctuaries on Sunday morning and subtract that number from the total seating capacity of those sanctuaries, we would get a collective picture of how over-propertied we are.

This is a hard one to figure out. Erecting buildings is hard and costly. The investment needed for a worshipping body to meet its need is immense. And there was a time when we had to build more and more sanctuaries, or expand ones we had already built—and at considerable expense. Our experience was that we couldn't build them fast enough. We would finish one, and it was full. Another one was needed.

But that's just not the case anymore in a post-baby boomer world. Very few of our sanctuaries are anywhere near full. Too much has happened in those spaces for people to let go of them easily. Communities are attached to them. It is going to be hard and painful to dissolve. Merging two churches in order to save space and money will be an unsavory prospect. And in denominations like the UCC, which have a congregational polity and where churches are fully autonomous, finding the leverage needed to persuade them to sell their property will not be easy.

And yet, our buildings are killing us. Ok—not all of them, but enough of them. We have to take a serious and collective look at this. This has to be on the table for discussion as we move forward as the Church. We have to develop a new narrative built around the centrality of mission, subjecting everything else to it.

Buildings must serve a clear missional purpose and must be funded and maintained in a way that mission is not sacrificed or impeded. You don't start that conversation by asking how much meaningful mission can we get by with and still keep the building. You start that conversation by knowing with passion what your mission is and then, objectively, at times heartlessly, asking whether or not the building will fulfill, enhance, or impede that mission.

If the building is an impediment for the sake of the mission, it may be important to free yourself from it and find a more creative way both to be church and to fund your mission. Some churches are doing just that. Without a collective will to engage critical church leaders in a broader conversation about this, I fear that underutilized property attached to churches in decline will continue to compromise our future health and vitality.

Postmodernity

If there is not enough good research on population shifts in America and their overall impact on church growth and sustainability, the same cannot be argued about what is a third critical factor contributing to church decline. It has to do with change.

Population studies are about numbers. Postmodernity is about culture, change within it, and an organization's ability to cope with that. There are thousands of good books, articles, blog sites, web sites, magazines and videos already produced about postmoderns and how they are changing what we once knew as Church. Among the more influential authors on this subject are Phyllis Tickle, Rob Bell, Anthony Robinson, Peter Rollins, Brian McClaren, Nadia Bolz Wever and so many others.

It is not my intention to argue about the impact that postmodernity is having on the Church. It is not my intention to write in great detail about what kind of impact it is having on the Church. I myself rely on others to do that for me, as I'm sure many of you do as well.

I do, however, want to highlight some of what I have learned about this cultural shift and make some observations about how the shift is contributing not just to church decline, but to the much harder reality to cope with—that some of our churches are going to die because of it.

I am going to narrow my focus here to three statements about postmoderns. I want to look closely at what they reveal about shifts in expectations regarding what it means to be a person of faith. There could, of course, be many more statements made about that. These are illustrative of the point I want to make, which is that change is coming fast, and is of such a substantive difference that some churches are going to die and others are going to have to be built anew to replace them. Not only have we saturated the market for a population base that isn't growing anymore; not only are we compromising our missional output by pouring dollars into properties that don't serve our mission, but a whole new worldview is emerging that makes much of what the Church of modernity was built to do obsolete.

These statements I am using suggest that the change that is called for is not just at the level of replacing something stale with something fresh, wondering what the cost will be and whether or not we can afford it. It is also not about whether or not we want to make that change. Therefore, I am not going to write about things like whether or not a church should replace their organ with electric guitars; whether or not the pastor should wear a robe; whether the pastor should preach from the pulpit; whether or not we should replace bulletins with big screens; whether or not we should add a contemporary service Those are changes at the technical level that completely miss the point. I am looking at what makes for a paradigm shift, the kind of change that requires whole new ways of thinking about what we do, for whom we do it, and why we do it. I am talking about what leadership studies call adaptive changes.

Statement One

Postmoderns do not believe that there is such a thing as universal truth; in other words, what is true for you may or may not be true for me.

This simple statement is a game changer for the Church. We have not even begun to wrap our heads and hearts around how deeply the Church as it has been known for two millennia now has invested in the notion that there are universal truths. Postmodernity doubts, if not outright denies, this.

Whether it is a fact or not that there are no universal truths is irrelevant. Well, of course it's relevant. But in this chapter about why some churches are going to die, that argument is moot. It's moot because two facts subsist side by side: postmoderns don't believe universal truths apply; many churches don't know how to teach or preach in the ambiguity that permeates a world with no universal truths.

For simplicity's sake, let's look at only one aspect of the Church of modernity: the role of clergy in the life of the institutional church.

I made a bold statement to the annual meeting delegates of the Southwest Conference three years ago at the Church of the Red Rocks in Sedona, Arizona. I said that in many of our churches full-time, seminary-trained, ordained clergy were already an impediment to the missional life of the Church.

That statement suggests two very different things.

It suggests that for many of our churches, the cost of maintaining a salary for these clergy is so prohibitive that they sacrifice their missional calling in order to keep paying a full-time pastor's salary. The smallest congregation I know of that pays a full-time pastor has around 25 members. I intend to imply that there are churches that ignore their missional calling without looking with a critical eye at how paying a full-time pastor (the average cost of which now exceeds $85,000—and for whom health care alone is close to $20,000) affects what mission they can actually undertake. This contributes to the ever-growing phenomenon that all that pastors are asked to undertake as their "mission" is to meet their congregants' needs.

Let's put aside the financial argument. When I talk about clergy being a missional impediment, I suggest something far more subtle than churches that can't afford the price tag of full-time clergy are sacrificing some of their missional calling by spending beyond their means to keep a pastor.

I also mean to suggest that what we have trained clergy to do and be is not what those whom we are trying to attract to church expect a pastor should be. That may even be an understatement. It may well be the case that the role of clergy, however it may come to define itself, is something that postmoderns aren't asking for in order to sustain their faith.

Clergy are well trained, well equipped, and well prepared to lead a church. With each passing year, that postmodern culture isn't producing enough followers who are asking for what they have been trained, equipped, and prepared to offer.

The Church of modernity upholds fundamental truths about theology, about morality, about lifestyle choices, about liturgical and ritual practices, about scripture, about sacraments. It invests in educating those who articulate and defend a call to ministry as a means of propagating and preserving those truths and standards from one generation to another. It prepares clergy to know full well what those truths and standards are. It examines them very carefully, and renders judgment about their fitness for ministry in and on its behalf. It tests whether they have the capacity to sustain those fundamental truths. It has to know whether someone authorized for ministry will or will not be a threat to its historic, traditional teachings, practices, and standards. It gives them a pulpit each week from which they speak as a trained expert on what they have learned, or about what God has inspired them to say. And it provides them every week with a passive audience to absorb that teaching.

This is not an argument for or against the merits of this model of being Church. It is simply an observation that as long as we invest in educating, training, and paying experts to speak on behalf of the Church, and in the speaking deploy them to maintain an established orthodoxy, we will have lost the postmoderns. In this changing environment that postmodernity is birthing, the role of clergy as trained, professional, authorized expert who speaks with the permission of and under the watchful eye of the mother Church could become an impediment to the overall mission of the Church.

This is a good time to point out that we are not talking here about a generation gap. This is not about asking what does this generation want and what we can do to accommodate them. Postmodernity is a movement that is expected to last as long as the age of modernity or Enlightenment did, about 500 years. What's at stake here is not finding out how to get teenagers back into Church. This is a question about what we can do to prevent moving from talk about some churches dying to talk about the Church dying.

That postmoderns do not buy into the notion of universal truth has a couple of important consequences. The first is that they are simply not going to invest in a model of the Church that asks an expert with the answers to talk to them while they remain passive.

Postmoderns come into every encounter with others believing that each person in the room has life experiences that make them wise. They want to know what those experiences have taught them, and expect that their own experiences will be valued in the conversation. They believe that only in a community that ritualizes open dialogue can we discover new truths. Architecture, liturgy, and ecclesiology that rely on the trained expert in the room to establish truth or morality will not capture their attention. Such a church will no longer be the Church of their heart.

One final note here: I don't want to go too far into writing an apologetic for postmoderns and their way of thinking. I really only want us to understand what are some of the elements of this paradigm shift so that we can begin to wrap our heads around why so much feels different to us. Having said that, I will point out that one of the observations made by postmoderns is that too much of what we now accept as truth is the byproduct of white heterosexual males having almost exclusive control over determining, defining, and establishing for everyone else what will be accepted as truth.

It should not surprise us that others have different ideas. Women raised in a world that viewed them as everything from inferior beings to nothing more than the legal property of their male head of household will have different perspectives on truth. It should not surprise us that one's sexual orientation can affect one's relationship with moral judgments made exclusively through the lenses of heterosexual males. It should not surprise us that those who are not white, many of whom lived through slavery and genocide at the hands of the white man, also construct different worldviews with different relationships to what has been established as universally true for all.

In the age of postmodernity, the filters of race, gender, sexual identity, culture, class, and income level all matter. In the end, this

17

may not be an argument so much about there not being universal truths applied across the board for all people throughout all of time. It may be much simpler than that. It is their observation that human intellect cannot escape the impact that race, gender, and other factors play in impeding the ability to recognize and articulate these universal truths without error. My relationship to truth will always be negotiated through lenses and filters, the impacts of which I cannot escape.

Statement Two
Postmoderns learn differently.

In the last two generations there has been an important epistemological shift. This is not an argument that they learn better, just that they learn differently. This is not something they chose to do or choose not to do, but is the byproduct of technological developments that impact the brain and how it processes stimuli. It is really important as we begin this discussion to realize that this is not a matter of choice. No child raised in postmodernity said, "I think that the way my parents and grandparents learned is outmoded. Sit me in front of a TV, computer, laptop, notebook, gaming device, and smartphone and condition my brain to learn differently." And yet, that is exactly what parents have done to their children for the last two generations. I don't make any judgments about that, I only take note of what others are now noticing about how the brain is affected by that, and then how that impacts the culture at large and the Church more particularly.

In his 1985 work *Amusing Ourselves to Death*, Neil Postman writes about a different intelligence capacity required by the print medium as opposed to film or television. He refers to Marshall McCluhan's oft-quoted phrase, "the medium is the message," and proffers instead this adage: "the medium is the metaphor."

Born in 1931, Postman represented the first generation to spend its childhood in front of a television. His landmark book was an attempt to understand just what television had done not just to entertain us but also to condition us as a culture to learn differently.

He noted that by the time the average child began her elementary school education, she had already spent more time in front of a TV than she would spend in the classroom by the time she graduated high school. He wrote about what the patterns endemic to the standard television program did to condition the brain to process outside stimuli. Those processes would have a profound effect on how a child learns.

These are averages, more close approximations than exact figures, but you will get the point. Every three seconds or so, the image on the TV screen changes. Every two minutes, give or take, the scene changes. Every seven and a half minutes the program takes a break, and over the next three and a half minutes nothing relative to the plot development occurs. In essence, a whole new narrative develops and is completed in thirty-second increments throughout those three and a half minutes. Then we return to the plot until another seven or eight minutes goes by, and we repeat the pattern of thirty-second interruptions. The entire plot narrative plays out in thirty to sixty minutes. There is drama, there is conflict, there is tension, and there is resolution.

Now, take that same child who for six years has been sitting either passively in front of that ever changing screen and set them in a classroom for eight hours a day where the scene doesn't change and one voice speaks minute after minute after minute.

They get bored easily. The brain has been conditioned to process stimuli in one way. It is used to an almost constantly changing scene. It expects some drama, some conflict, some resolution (entertainment, shall we say). It has been wired to learn differently. Under these new circumstances, it might learn something, but not nearly enough of what we had come to expect from students raised under a very different set of circumstances.

The very first time I heard the phrase "paradigm shift" was in 1990. I was attending a seminar for schoolteachers. They were all being introduced to a whole new educational model. These were men and women who had been trained as professionals. They were very good at what they did. In spite of being very good at it, they noticed, with some frustration, that what they were doing wasn't working.

The superintendent of the school district invited _ part in the training. While there, one m~ clearly: we don't learn the way we t this, but whole new methods of lea. to have to be developed. Your own to be a teacher, a job you have beer years, is of little use to you. If our mi: ways aren't educating, then new wa must emerge. That was the first tim

paradigm shifts. That was the first time I had to wrap my head around the difference between technical shifts and adaptive changes. That was the first time I realized that we were not talking any more about subtle changes, but substantive ones that were going to be very hard to make.

Educational systems have worked hard to make those changes. The Church has not. That day was an epiphany to me. In the 23 years that have followed, I have pursued at varying degrees of success the call to transform the Church as we know it. There is a gospel to be proclaimed, to be sure. How do we do that if our methods of proclaiming it aren't communicating effectively? What does it mean when the medium, not the message, must change?

Clergy who think that a 30-45 minute monologue is our most effective way of teaching are deluding themselves. Folk are listening, but they aren't necessarily learning. Typically, our brains are checking in and out every couple of minutes or so. Those who can focus with intention and discipline will stay in the game longer than others, but our brains aren't conditioned to learn anymore by listening to one voice, watching one face, and following one train of thought for much longer than a few minutes. We take our own breaks during these monologues, wonder around for a while, and come back. Sometimes the break is only a few seconds. Sometimes it is a few minutes later. Sometimes, they don't come back at all. This happens now for even those most invested in the life of the Church. For countless others, this modality of being Church is not something they have a willingness to invest in anymore. It simply doesn't meet their needs.

This is not a rejection of the Church as Church. This is not a denial of the value of a life well lived, enhanced by meaningful encounters with the sacred and shaped by like-minded people living in a committed community of faith with one another. It is simply the experience of coming to church, wanting to have a meaningful encounter, and walking out under-stimulated, bored, and having arned little to nothing.

This single epistemological shift, a direct result of sitting en in front of the television, the computer, the notebook, the hone—is a game changer. Schools are adapting, but by and ches are not.

t a judgment about one way being better than another. 't stupid. They learn differently, but they learn. They adapt. They meet the needs of a changing world. Almost everywhere they go, they find the world a curious, inviting, and interesting place that has changed with them. Until they get to church.

I spend much of my time listening to pastors and lay leaders who love their churches. Their lives have been transformed by their experiences there. They are willing to sacrifice a great deal to help make that happen for others. One of their familiar refrains, borne largely from the grief of seeing a beloved church in decline, is that mega-churches, evangelicals, and fundamentalists attract so many because all they do is entertain. This refrain misses the point (it also fails to notice that the decline we are experiencing is having as deep an impact on all churches birthed in the age of modernity, regardless of their theological or ecclesiological background). The point is that brains are wired a bit differently today than they were two or three generations ago. Others are adapting to this because they recognize that their mission can be achieved regardless of the medium.

The Church all too often confuses the medium with the message. It assumes that abandoning centuries old liturgical practices for the sake of modern expediencies is tantamount to dumbing down the gospel. Whether you use a thirty-minute sermon or a well-produced 15 minute video, if the message is well-crafted you have the potential to produce the same end result.

I don't mean to suggest that churches need to invest in big screens, rock bands, noise, or entertainment quality Christianity. What I do mean to suggest is that a stubborn, self-righteous insistence that our medium is as sacred as our message is one of the factors contributing to our demise. And in some instances, an unwillingness to ask deeper questions about how to translate message with new media will be revealed in the post-mortems of some of our once vital and healthy churches.

In essence, and with some notable exceptions, progressive Christianity has ceded relevant Christianity to our more fundamentalist, conservative partners in faith who don't have any issues with using a variety of media to proclaim their message. The noise may attract for a while, but even postmoderns who find the theology of most mega-churches too narrow are walking away. We simply aren't yet giving them a choice to hear our message proclaimed in a way that they have been conditioned to receive it.

Cameron Trimble, Executive Director of the Center for Progressive Christianity, puts it this way: "While conservative churches are less flexible with their theology, they are incredibly adaptable when it comes to their ritual and liturgy. Progressive Christianity, on the other hand, is has a very flexible theology, but refuses to change its ritual and liturgy."

We learn differently today. Old forms no longer serve as well as they once did. The longer the Church I love fails to adapt wisely to these changes—and we are already at least one generation late to this game—the more of our churches are going to die. I do grieve this—though perhaps not with the intensity of some others I know. I do not want the grief over these deaths to disable the Church I love from making the important and necessary changes required to remain relevant for the sake of our mission and our message.

Statement Three
Postmoderns do not trust institutional authority.
One of the lessons my father relied heavily upon in raising me was to trust authority. It came out in aphorisms like "trust your elders;" "respect adults;" "don't question the Church;" "whether you like it or not, do what you are told by those in power." By the time I reached adulthood, it was clear to me that to succeed in my dad's world, an unquestioning submission to authority was a given.

I couldn't bring myself to pass those lessons on to my children. In fact, I told them to question everything and everyone, regardless of their status, power, or position.

That's a big shift in attitude, orientation, and perception.

I spent eight years in the Catholic seminary. From whatever age it is that a child begins to think about her future, I knew I was called to be a priest. I remember sitting in the classroom of my Catholic grade school when the parish priest came in to talk about vocation. He asked if any of us had ever thought about serving the Church. It was the first time I was ever given a chance to name publicly what I had known in my heart for a long time. I immediately and enthusiastically raised my hand. Though I was surprised by the responses of my classmates, my teacher, and even to a certain extent the priest (let's just say I wasn't the most well-behaved student), I was not in any way deterred from pursuing what I felt was a call to the priesthood.

This isn't a story about my vocational pathway, but about what happened to me after grade school. I spent eight years in seminary preparing for the priesthood. Against the advice of my father, I started questioning everything and everyone. There was no calculation in

22

this for me. This was not a generational rebellion. This was not a conscious effort to eschew the ways of my father and define myself in my own terms.

It was an intellectual curiosity. It was a pursuit of deeper knowledge. It was an effort prior to ordination to know why I was being asked to believe what the church was teaching me. That was in part for my own sake, but also for the sake of those to whom, upon ordination, I would be entitled to dictate what they could and could not believe.

I would soon learn that I walked in what was the church and the world of my father. My worldview was already different that the one I now lived in. In this old paradigm, there were no questions. Authority spoke, and when it did the matter was settled. Invariably, I got the same response to every question: "John, these are the teachings of the church. They have been this way for 2,000 years. Who are you to question them?"

That led, after eight years, to a heartbreaking decision not to seek ordination as a Catholic priest. I decided that I could not, with any kind of integrity, have hands laid upon me by the same bishop who would require of me a vow of obedience. Once I took that vow, I was obligated to require others to believe what he asked, knowing that I didn't yet fully believe it.

My story is not an unfamiliar one. I am a boomer who learned that it was not only permissible to question authority; it was a cultural requirement and expectation.

Boomers came of age in the aftermath of significant global upheaval. World War II saw an overt attempt to wipe out a significant part of the human community. Over 6 million Jews were annihilated in a genocide that gave us all new insight into our capacity for sustaining evil. In a single moment, "Little Boy" was dropped off the Enola Gay over Hiroshima and seconds later 70,000 people were dead. Almost every morning of my childhood I watched a war unfold in Southeast Asia. I saw dead and maimed bodies. I also listened to the rhetoric of a nation that could no longer articulate a narrative that made sense of the bloody mess we were watching. To the contrary, the voices I came to respect were calling into question everything that America thought it stood for. At the same time, I saw two Kennedy's and a King assassinated while bigots and racists turned firehouses and attack dogs on my neighbors. As I left my childhood years and entered my teens, I watched my president resign in shame. I sat glued to the TV day after day watching Sam Ervin interrogate Mitchell, Dean, Liddy, Hunt and everyone else who conspired to end democracy, as we knew it.

There was no moment of epiphany. I never sat down and said "time to question authority." I just absorbed the world around me. Everything would be questioned.

By that time, I fashioned myself a bit of a rebel. "Question authority" had become my motto. My heroes were the rebels, including all of the great prophets from our canon, whose words stung the powerful elite of their time. I saw judicatory work as compliance with power structures against which I had now committed myself to fight.

By the time of my ordination, I was a by-product not of a generational shift but of a paradigm shift I had no deep capacity to yet fully understand. That's a way of saying that the middle to the end of the twentieth century will be marked as a turning point in history.

Among the many things that have shifted in the age of postmodernity is a posture towards authority and institution. We have built a model of church that has sustained the gospel well and served the needs of its mission well. Buttressed by clearly delineated lines of authority and power, the church has maintained a level of excellence for which it should be proud. I know of horrors committed throughout the ages by the abuse of power and authority—that is another subject for another time.

The world has shifted a bit, and after the schism that is postmodernity, we sit on the other side of the shift and realize that postmoderns don't orient the same way towards authority.

I actually think this is going to be the hardest change with which the Church must cope. Everything about our way of being assumes that authority is identified, prepared, examined, and empowered.

Bylaws tell us who can act on another's behalf and under what circumstances. They grant power and authority to some people, for some time, and under some circumstances. Committees that are duly elected process, prepare, study, examine, vote, and determine. Clergy are called, educated, examined, and authorized. Bishops, Conference Ministers, Presbyters, Elders, Deacons, Regional Ministers and authority figures of all kinds preside over defined geographies. Ordination requires a comprehensive examination by trained people who have proven both a dedication to the institution and an understanding of their role in perpetuating core values.

I do not mean to suggest that there is anything wrong with this. That is not my point. I have learned to function very well in this system and have been given a position of authority because of it. I have also, to a certain extent, gained critical insight into the purpose of these structures to support our mission.

But I am from a generation who heard over and over again that authority can be trusted. That is not true of my children.

The Church I serve isn't going to stop examining, testing, and educating clergy. They aren't going to throw out their bylaws. They aren't going to stop electing members to serve on committees and empowering the committees to make decisions for the good of the whole. Authority will be identified, prepared, examined, and empowered. This structure will continue to support the missional life of the Church I know and love.

What are we going to do with those communities of faith that are springing up all over the place, though, who have no relationship to our established and recognized authority? Spiritual guides are calling people into the faith with no training, no examination, and no authorization. Who records their baptisms? Who tests whether or not their ritual meets with our established standards? Who examines, lays hands on, and keeps oversight of their pastors? Who tests the boundaries of our recognized orthodoxies and dogmas when these independent, free-thinkers function without oversight or accountability?

Even through the time of the Reformation, the Protestant church brought with it a need to establish lines of authority for the sake of our missional and sacramental life. Postmoderns just aren't buying into that way of structuring their lives. Ordained clergy may or may not have meaning to them. Even if they do, using ordained clergy as the empowered experts in the room to address the questions of the day will most certainly not have any meaning to them. Becoming a "member" in order to acquire voting rights and be permitted to serve an elected position of authority will most likely not have any meaning to them. Attaching themselves to denominational structures that have to be funded and obeyed will likely not have any meaning, either.

All that the Church has relied upon to maintain its orthodoxy, to guarantee the safe deliverance of the faith from one generation to another within accepted limits and boundaries, is up for grabs. Churches of the modern era belong to denominations whose clergy have been trained and examined, whose leaders have been called, chosen, elected, appointed by others with recognized authority. We go back generations and can account for baptisms, confirmations, weddings, and deaths. In one generation, all of that is up for grabs.

We will struggle mightily with this. But that will be our problem. A whole new way of discovering the life of faith is emerging without the permission of, or training required by, the established Church. Those engaged in this faith exploration aren't asking for permission.

That is not an act of defiance. It is simply an awareness that our commitments to those matters consume too much of our time to make them see us as relevant. Their spiritual hungers are both asking for something more fulfilling and finding it in other places. They are not asking us for a fight over this. They don't want to change us. They simply have discovered that what their heart sings for is found somewhere other than in a church that, to their sensitivities, is over-committed to a reliance on authority.

These characteristics of the postmodern world contribute greatly to the decline of the Church of modernity: skepticism about universal truths; a different way of learning; and a built-in mistrust of authority. They are not really on the table for debate. Postmoderns are not interested in arguing with the modern world about who is right and who is wrong. They just happen to live in a world where expectations, assumptions, and perceptions have changed. They also happen to experience the Church of the modern world as incapable of making the kind of changes necessary to meet their vastly different spiritual hungers.

This has been a quick, and albeit very insufficient, look at what postmodernity hath wrought. We can fight it, but we will be tilting at windmills. It is.

As I said at the beginning of this chapter, the causes of the Church's diminishment in membership and financial contributions are many and their interplay is complex. We have looked here at only three of them: a critical decline in the birthrate; the cost of maintaining aging and underutilized buildings; and postmodernity.

There is much to be said about what all of this means to the Church I love, and in large part that is what the rest of his book will be about. Here I simply make the observation that some of our churches are going to die. These and other causes will conspire to close some of our churches.

The purpose of this chapter isn't simply to warn the Church that some pain is coming. It is a call to think differently about those coming deaths. As I close this chapter, I want to introduce the reader to what I have been calling "death with dignity."

If we can accept that some churches are going to die; if we can trust the capacity of our faith to sustain us through the grief and the pain that will come every time one does; and it we can shift our strategic approach to these deaths from reactive to proactive (meaning we have to be honest in our assessments with church leaders about their future); then we can have a very different kind of conversation about death.

Holy Ghost United Church of Christ was the oldest church in the St. Louis Association. It was clear that they, like many aging, white urban churches were in serious decline. Over three years of conversation with their elected and called leadership, I talked with them very seriously about all of their options.

We talked about using their existing resources to keep the doors open for as long as possible. We strategized about what could be cut in order to maximize the good use of their remaining assets and to ensure that those who had been members of that church for more than two generations could be buried from there.

We talked about merging with another church in the St. Louis area. We met with leaders from various churches about what that would look like.

We talked about closing the church. This would require actions taken by the leaders to satisfy legal expectations regarding the distribution of the remaining assets held by a not-for-profit corporation. It would also require them to respond to the ongoing need of their shut-ins and hospitalized. We also talked about which churches would be open to accepting the transfers of their remaining members.

Although all of these options were painful ones to talk about, this last one was initially the most painful one for them to think about.

I am grateful for a pastor who not only served that church with great love and skill, but who kept the leaders at the table in conversation even knowing how hard it was going to be for them.

Gertrude Scheible was well into her 90s when I met her. She was the grandmother at Holy Ghost for every child who came through there and, for almost 70 years, served as a Sunday School teacher. She attended faithfully every gathering of the St. Louis Association.

She had a perpetual smile on her face. She was the face of Holy Ghost Church. She was at every meeting I held with the lay leaders of that church and listened with an open heart to everything that was discussed. She prayerfully considered all options, including closing the church.

It took three years, but Gertrude and the leadership began to focus on what death with dignity might look like.

They began to realize that in order to fulfill the missional vision of those who built that church for a purpose; it might be their Christian duty to bring this congregation's life to an end, but an end with a purpose, a mission, if you will.

I will never forget the Sunday morning we gathered for the last time in the Sanctuary of Holy Ghost. With pride and dignity, the Moderator stood before the worshippers—many of whom hadn't been back in years and who traveled great distances to say their goodbyes and share cherished memories. The Moderator had taken great care to send invitations to many covenant partners beyond the membership of the church.

Before we would ritually decommission the church and offer words of closure, she carefully took time and, one by one, called those invited guests forward. To a children's home built to care for orphans she gave a check. To a woman's abuse shelter the same, as well as to the camp run by the Conference, and to the local Habitat for Humanity affiliate. All in all, about a dozen different missional partners were there to receive what was left of the church's assets.

Two moments from that service are forever indelibly marked in my memory. A representative of the St. Louis Historical Society was there to receive a gift from the church. Not money—something far more precious. As the first German Evangelical church in St. Louis was formed for and built by the new immigrants to the city, they were the recipients at their founding of a Bible written in the German script and given to them by Kaiser Wilhelm, the first German Emperor. His signature and prayerful inscription were penned inside the front cover. With white gloves covering his hands, the representative of the historical society came forward to carry that sacred text from the sanctuary to the archives of the city.

Then Gertrude stood up. Interrupting the ceremony and the decorum of the morning, breaking into this well-choreographed liturgy, she announced proudly: "I've been doing this for almost 70 years now, and I see no reason to stop. Would the children please come with me for their final lesson?" She walked out with the handful of children who had come on that last day of worship.

This church chose to die with dignity. I still remember that closing service as one of the most moving and beautiful I have ever had the pleasure of presiding over. I will never forget it. They helped me understand what resurrection life was all about. They died so that new life could emerge. After closing their accounts and sharing their missional resources with the Body of Christ, they kept a small council of leaders together to complete the sale of their property. The assets from that sale were given to the Missouri Mid-South Conference and were dedicated to new church starts.

To be sure, there was pain in this. But there was also a mature faith that refused to see death as the last word. Their leadership, their act of faith, served both as an inspiration to many and as a source of missional income to a few others.

It is now a part of my cache of options when visiting with church leaders who are facing decline and an uncertain future that at some point, and hopefully at the right point, we talk about death with dignity as a viable and a hope-filled option. Not every community is open to having that discussion—but many are.

Some of our churches are going to die.

Some of them will have an opportunity to approach that sacred moment with dignity.

CHAPTER TWO

Missional Resources

"If we have no peace, it is because we have forgotten we belong to each other."

- Mother Teresa

The Church was birthed for mission.
The word "mission" derives from the Latin verb *mittere*, to send. To be in mission is to be sent. The Church was birthed for a sending:

"Whom shall I send?" (Is. 6:8)

"I will also make you a light for the Gentiles, that my salvation may reach to the ends of the earth." (Acts 13:47)

"After this the Lord appointed seventy-two others and sent them.... He told them, 'The harvest is plentiful, but the workers are few. Ask the Lord of the harvest, therefore, to send out workers into his harvest field. Go! I am sending you....'" (Luke 10:1)

"Go, therefore, to all the ends of the earth." (Mark 16:15)

At the heart of what it means to be Church is a sending. But to where? And for what? At the heart of what it means to be Church is a sending. But to where? And for what? The man I call my spiritual father, the Rev. Dr. Sam Mann, talks about hearing the cries. When he does so, he intentionally calls our attention to this formational passage from Exodus 3:7-10:

The Lord said, "I have indeed seen the misery of my people in Egypt. I have heard them crying out because of their slave drivers, and I am concerned about their suffering. So I have come down to rescue them from the hand of the Egyptians and to bring them up out of that land into a good and spacious land, a land flowing with milk and honey— the home of the Canaanites, Hittites, Amorites, Perizzites,

Hivites and Jebusites. And now the cry of the Israelites has reached me, and I have seen the way the Egyptians are oppressing them. So now, go. I am sending you to Pharaoh to bring my people the Israelites out of Egypt."

In this passage from Exodus 3, we see the deep connection between a hearing of the cries and a sending forth. Moses is sent. Moses is given a mission in direct response to the cries of the people.

In every age and in every place, the Church is built for mission, for its sending. The great exodus was the response both of the discerning ear of God, who found the cries of the oppressed intolerable, and of the voice of that God calling for one to be sent.

Those with whom God has formed covenant are sent. Those with ears to hear must hear. "I have heard them crying out...." Those with eyes to see must see. "I have indeed seen the misery of my people...." And like the God with whom they have formed this covenant, the hearing and the seeing offer their voice to call forth meaningful, active, engaged action, looking for those willing to be sent, to be in mission: "I have come down to rescue them and bring them up."

Discernment, the art of listening, the spiritual discipline of hearing, be it the cries of the people or the voice of one crying in the wilderness or the invitation of God the Liberator sending us forth, is fundamental to undertaking mission. It is the art of hearing the cries. It is the discipline of discerning those cries and knowing to whom we are being sent, and for what purpose. It is the responsibility of the Church, and those who are in covenant with it, to discern what mission call sends them out. It is incumbent upon the leaders of our churches to articulate the clear missional purposes for which the Church was built.

We all know that every church, in this artful dance of discernment, takes into account a great number of factors. Every church will hear a multiplicity of voices crying out. Some of those voices will be unique to the community in which a church has been built. Some of the voices will be heard, but may have needs a given church is ill-prepared to meet. Every church has a limited number of resources they can use to respond to the cries that call them into mission: (financial, real estate, buildings, bodies, talents, time, etc.). Every church has partners in mission who may already be responding to a particular cry with skill, and whose expertise a church can draw on to be more effective and efficient.

Discernment requires skillful, prayerful, artful, playful listening.

Hunger; poverty; violence; abuse; loneliness; incarceration; oppression; war; disease; anxiety; depression: which cries are calling for us to be sent? What will this sending require of us?

Mission.

A sending forth.

One simple mantra reveals the core of my ecclesiology: it is about mission.

The Church is about one thing: its mission. We are called into being for a purpose. We are invited to be in mission. We are sent forth by a God with a vision for what this world could be, and who, in hope of fulfilling that vision, has always honored humanity with the invitation to participate in mission.

Owning one's mission with clarity, with passion, with purpose, and with intention is, I believe, what will keep the Church alive and vital and relevant. It is where the Spirit invests herself. She moves with her own impulses and purpose. She invites churches, their leaders and members to trust her and to go where they are sent.

Our Business is Mission

The Church is birthed for mission.

Peter Drucker, a man who has done consulting with churches for a long time now, always asks two questions: what is your business? And, how's business?

Speaking for the Church, I will argue that our business is mission. How's business? Well, there's the rub.

If asked to name the primary cause of the Church's malaise today, I would argue it is that we have abandoned a core, foundational sense of calling to mission. It is my observation that those churches that have a clear sense of what their mission is are strong, healthy, and vital. That won't be true in every case since, of course, other factors matter. The centrality of mission as a core organizing principle, however, cannot be overrated; and is often simply absent from too many churches.

Too many churches, though, have forgotten how essential mission is to their identity and their reason for being. Mission has become, for many churches, what gets done with the money left over after all the bills have been paid.

Ask anyone who has been active in the Church for a while, when your church cuts its budget, what is the first thing that gets cut? Most people will tell you its some piece of their mission budget.

I walk into church after church after church and ask them what their mission is and, with very few exceptions, I get very confused responses. It isn't so much that they don't know what their mission is. It is much more the case that they don't realize that it is imperative or necessary to have one.

There is a church in the Southwest Conference that is thriving. It is one of the healthiest, most mature, vital churches I know. It is an unapologetically progressive community of faith in one of the most conservative parts of America: southern Arizona just about thirty miles north of the border between the U.S. and Mexico.

The first time I worshipped with them, their pastor, the Rev. Dr. Randy Mayer, stood up and, with a smile on his face and so much pride and conviction, announced, "We are a church on the border, called to serve the immigrant."

No one in that church, packed for the second time that Sunday to the deepest edges of the sanctuary, was unaware of that. They knew for what reason God called them into the desert to be Church.

Every day, they send out jeeps with volunteers to drive through the desert. They look for migrants who, though dying in the desert in disgustingly high numbers, hope for a better way to feed their families and believe what they hear about America being the place to do that. These church members place water in the desert. They negotiate differences between immigrants and the border patrol. They hold workshops and seminars and training events with some of this country's most intelligent men and women, teaching gringos the truth about border politics and policies, about the causes of migration, about the impact of the wall on our psyche, the environment, and relationships with our otherwise peaceful neighbors to the south. They sit in courtrooms when migrants are processed through our judicial system. They write their elected representatives constantly about drones on the border and a myriad of other political hot potatoes that few other churches would touch.

This is a church with a mission. This is a church with a purpose. This is a church whose members know when they join that they will be sent into the desert. They hear the cries. They witness the misery. They embrace their mission.

This is Church as it was meant to be. They can't stop growing. I know there are many churches like this. I celebrate every one.

Let's be honest, though. Too many churches have forgotten how absolutely central mission is to their lifeblood. For me, it really is this simple: the Spirit will invest herself in those places where there is a clear mission.

It has been my experience of late that too many churches have slipped into an undeclared mission that can be reduced to this: save our Church. At all costs, no matter what it takes, keep the doors open. Meetings are reduced to discussions about the membership and the budget. Membership drives have become in many places the byproduct of a strategy to feed the budget. It's as if our evangelistic zeal reduces our call to extending an invitation that sounds something like this: "Hey, if you're looking for a church to join, why not try ours? We fell short of budget last year, and could use a few dozen more to contribute to our bottom line. Mind if I take a look in your wallet?"

Churches face the daunting prospect of fully funding staff and property. Endowments often get tapped to cover the losses in membership contributions and budget deficits.

While all that is happening, money for mission gets cut. After all, churches have to have a pastor. Churches have to maintain buildings and property. The hungry, or the poor, or the prisoners, or college campus ministries, or support for the denomination, or the abused will all have to find some other way to raise their money. Church officers were elected to maintain the organizational needs of this church. Leaders are called upon to think deeply about what it will take to perpetuate the life of a church they have come to love. No one stops to ask why it is the Spirit needs the Church anymore. It is just assumed that elected leadership bears the burden of not letting the church close on their watch.

Not for nothing—this is one of the most significant behaviors witnessed and named by those who today see the Church as irrelevant. Postmoderns want to know that their life's energy will be spent on something meaningful. They want to be called into action. They want to know that they are needed. They want to experience something transformative. They want to know that you see something in them that is of value and that you know how to make use of it for the common good. Being elected or appointed to serve on a committee and deliberate about how to finance or fund a dying institution has no appeal to them. They want to be sent. More often than not these days they experience the Church as unable, or worse unwilling, to offer that to them.

In the last chapter, I wrote about the burden that aging property can be on church budgets. We have reached a point in many of our churches where, instead of subjecting the property to the mission, mission is subjected to the needs of the property. Either the building has become the mission by default, since it consumes the lion's share of the budgetary outgo, or what outreach mission there is must conform to what the building allows.

Covenant and Mission

If your denomination, like mine, is one wherein the churches own the property and the churches function with complete autonomy, the argument I am about to make will be a difficult one to defend. Even if it can be defended, it will be all the more difficult to do anything about. I make it anyway.

Missional assets and resources belong to the body of Christ, the Church collectively. Especially in times of diminishing resources, the appropriate allocation of our collective assets is essential. An organizational model that sees local churches as independent, autonomous franchises has been one way of imagining that the collective mission of the Church can be lived out more faithfully and efficiently. The collective assets are to be stewarded with a clear sense of missional calling always at the forefront.

Seen as fully independent bodies, local churches are empowered in this model of the Church to make isolated decisions about the missional assets they control. There is, with each passing year, not only less and less of a commitment to funding the mission of the wider Church, there are fewer and fewer church leaders left who even understand why that is necessary in the first place. This is especially true of churches who own their property and who are engaged in dialogue about the missional value and/or contribution of that property. Judicatory leaders, wider Church representatives, and covenant partners who are not a part of that church's fellowship are not invited into that conversation. It has been said of my United Church of Christ that, when our epitaph is written, the gravestone will have but one word on it: autonomy.

When autonomy, the desire to be free of outside constraint, is not balanced with covenant, the impulse to attach to one's independence a call to serve the greater good, then autonomy is seen mistakenly as independence *from* something rather than *for* something. The collective and shared missional commitment of the wider Church is compromised under these circumstances.

When I served on staff for the Missouri Mid-South Conference, I looked at a map of the greater St. Louis area. I could see vast cathedral-style churches throughout the urban core of that city. These were inspiring, beautiful churches. And they were sitting largely empty on Sunday.

The churches had mostly part-time staff serving sporadically, with little activity going on in the buildings during the week. There were pockets of vital, strong, and active churches, but surrounding them were covenant partners who were barely hanging on.

I initiated conversations with leaders in the association inviting us all to sit down with a map, count the churches, the number of members worshipping in each one, the seating capacity of each of them, and the distances separating them. The idea was to assess together how many sanctuaries we needed given the number of worshippers that were active and how far each could travel. Then, we would talk openly about which churches we would close, which properties would be sold, how the active members could be redistributed to meet everyone's best interests, and how the assets would be better utilized in the fulfillment of our mission.

That conversation never took hold. It wasn't that leaders in the association didn't see the wisdom in such a conversation. It was more that they felt that intruding on a local church's right to make those decisions independent of outside interference was sacrosanct. It was felt that protecting the autonomy of each local church was a greater good than risking conversation about what it means to be in mission partnership as one and what that partnership might make possible if we saw our resources and assets as property commonly shared for the sake of our mission.

I am arguing here that all missional assets belong to the Church, not in a legal sense, but in a missional sense. I accept autonomy as a good. I support the independence that churches and their elected officers have to make good decisions. I also think that independence without covenant is not healthy. Such an arrangement does not serve the missional calling of the Church. The longer churches remain siloed entities, blissfully ignorant of how their decisions impact the wider Church, the longer the Church as a whole will suffer the consequences.

Churches steward their resources not only for the sake of their members but also for the sake of the mission for which the Church was birthed. This is my belief. Autonomous bodies must remain in full covenant partnership with a host of others. I am arguing that churches that sit largely empty every Sunday are called upon to assess the extent to which the assets they control are serving the Church and its mission.

If we can't learn to play together this way, we're going to continue to waste assets that aren't doing everything they can for our shared mission. "Where two or more are gathered" was an assurance that God's Holy Spirit will abide when we come together as brothers and sisters, no matter the number or circumstances. It was not an argument that handful of people worshipping in a sanctuary that seats 300 have a moral obligation to preserve that space for those who built it 250 years ago.

Trust the Spirit

For me, this isn't an academic pursuit or an argument made in a vacuum. As we transition from one way of being Church to another, the question of missional assets is a real one. One of the reasons I wrote this book was to help the current expression of the Church to understand two things. The first is that the Church that is coming arises out of the clear movement of God's Holy Spirit. The second is that we have an obligation to assess how many of our missional resources are to be invested in birthing this new way of being Church.

I need to say more about both of those statements.

I have spent much of my time serving the United Church of Christ in the Southwest learning everything I can about what Cameron Trimble calls church 3.0 (the church of the first century and beyond being church 1.0, the Reformation Church being church 2.0, and the postmodern church being church 3.0). I am grateful that I serve in a conference that gives me that freedom.

In my second year as conference minister, our board committed to a full year of visioning. In the middle of the year, and while personally working with a brilliant executive coach, I undertook a study of how my time was being used for the sake of our mission.

We discovered that 96 percent of my time was going to what we categorized as "maintenance." Make no mistake; we did not underestimate the importance of a judicatory office working to maintain the life of our existing churches. That is very important.

During a time when we were talking about our vision for the future, about long range goals and about restructuring to support those goals, it became clear to us that we would be sacrificing our future and our vision if the leader spent 96% of his time maintaining what already existed. After a great deal of deliberation, the board decided that my goal should be to spend 50% of my time on maintenance, and 50% of my time on visioning work.

I chose to come to this conference precisely because of this. A telling piece of the conference's own birth narrative is that these 25 churches became a conference in 1965 when they petitioned our national governing convention to split from a conference that included Southern California. With only 25 churches in what would be our new geography (covering Arizona, New Mexico and El Paso, Texas), it wasn't a given that the national delegates would vote to give us that independence.

But they did. In the document we wrote to the delegates to support our claim for becoming our own conference, the opening line reads: "Given our size and potency, our gift to the denomination will be the gift of experimentation."

It was in that spirit that in 2009, some 44 years after that promise, the Board of the Southwest Conference voted to call its leader to spend half of his time doing visioning work. And that is precisely what I have committed myself to do ever since.

A part of that is learning what I can about church 3.0. Later in the book, I am going to write about some settings where this way of being Church is being lived out. I am going to share with you what I have experienced first hand in leaving the world of church 2.0 for a while and discovering what it is many of us have been hearing about around the edges for some time.

For now, let me say this with clarity: what I have come to witness, and what I have experienced, leads me to believe that whatever the Spirit is doing here—She can be trusted. I have no doubt that what is emerging all over the Church is not only something new, but something authentic. When I say authentic, I mean a true response to a missional calling of the Holy Spirit. I mean a true sending forth to meet a real need.

Too many of us live with the fear that the emergence of this new way of being Church means the death of the old. We see this as a zero sum game. I don't believe that. I believe that for quite some time, the Body of Christ will see the need for a church 2.0 and a church 3.0, just as after the Reformation Church 1.0 did not disappear. Having said that, I think the changes that postmodernity will bring will diminish over the next century just how many churches 2.0 the world will need, but church 2.0 isn't going to disappear.

In the first chapter we talked about what the onset of postmodernity has meant. There are many for whom the current expression of the Church is simply not going to feed their spiritual hunger.

It is my conviction that the Holy Spirit is birthing something new for this time. Churches may be dying—and as I said, some will die. The cause of those deaths is not the emergence of something new. There are other factors at play regarding the death of some churches and the diminishment of others. It is also true that many of our strong, healthy, vital, and mission-minded churches are going to be around for a long time.

A New Missional Partner

This brings me to the second point, which is really what this whole chapter on missional resources is about. The call to inventory our collective assets and the call to see them as a part of the Church universal isn't just about doing what we can to save church 2.0. Ultimately, it is a call to the Church as we know it to ask serious questions about how many of our current assets already rightfully belong to a church in its infancy.

There is a radical shift that has to take place—and soon.

The Church that exists is, I sincerely believe, invited to see the Church that is emerging as its missional partner. Too many of the leaders of the Church to which I belong see church 3.0 as a threat. In a time where fear about the future of their local church or their denomination predominates and immense grief and anxiety fester, it is very easy for us to perceive the new church as the cause of that grief and anxiety. They have become for many of us the scapegoat.

I have given myself to the task of writing this book to church 2.0 as a way of hoping against hope that this will change. I believe that a beautiful partnership can exist when both church 2.0 and church 3.0 see each other as missional partners with a shared call to preach the gospel. We will do it very differently, to be sure. So long as we see each other as threats, the mission for which we were birthed suffers.

Every October, all authorized ministers in the Southwest Conference gather for retreat. Our clergy play together so well; watching them enjoy each other's company during this retreat is one of my profound joys.

Last year, we spent our time talking about the church 3.0. There was some pain, some grief, and some anxiety felt and expressed amongst the clergy. Many of them don't know for how much longer their church can afford to keep them. They are literally worried about how much longer they are going to be able to earn an income.

On the second night of the retreat, we invited an emergent pastor to come worship with us.

She entered the room terrified. She had no training. She had no authorization. She had no denominational support or oversight. She was in a room of experts and was being asked to "lead worship" for us. We would discover that worship was our language, not hers. She couldn't say that what she did would qualify as worship.

She told us that every Sunday, anywhere from 9 to 40 people gather in her home. They have accepted her as their spiritual guide. She typically takes about two hours before they gather to think and pray about what to do when they get there. She confessed that for the "experts" she perceived us to be, she considered spending considerably more time than that. In the end, she thought better of it and decided that she would be her authentic self.

It was fascinating to me to watch the ordained clergy sit in a chapel in conversation with this woman. I could see quickly that whatever they imagined before about threat, about anger, about anxiety, was fast dissipating as they listened to her.

She set up a rudimentary altar. On it were various objects that had no relation to one another. There were candles, books, plants, toys, children's drawings, tchotchkes of varying color and shape all strewn about.

She asked us all to go and gather at our leisure around that table and just linger until our spirit was invited to focus on one object. We did this with no resistance and with no more direction than that. She brought with her a musician who played guitar and sang gently behind us while we followed her direction. When we were finished, she invited us to share what caught our attention and to risk sharing what story emerged because of that.

What happened was precious, sacred, and beautiful. It was, dare I say, worshipful. The presence of the sacred was unmistakable.

When we finished, she sat with us for another hour and took questions. I will tell her story later. This is a story about us—about those of us who experience this new and emergent reality with wonder, fear, and anxiety.

Something changed that night. One of the stories she told was about a couple that asked her to do a baptism. That frightened her. She had no idea what to do. She told us, though, that in two weeks she would figure it out and do that baptism.

I mention that for this reason: by the time she left that night, there wasn't a single authorized minister in the room who doubted that whatever she did, it would be authentic. That baptism was going to "count," whatever that means.

It is also true that no one doubted that night that what we did was sacred, genuine, and authentic.

It is also true that no one doubted that, when that group gathered in her home every Sunday, they were the Church.

And so I ask: is it better that we ask her and her followers to conform somehow, someway, to what we have built the Church to be; or to trust that the Spirit is doing something with her for the sake of our shared mission?

Given all that I have come to experience about what we loosely refer to as the Church emergent, or that I have come to call church 3.0, I have resolved that question with a firm conviction that not only is what is coming authentic and birthed by the impulse of Holy Spirit, but also that those of us who steward missional assets have a covenant obligation to discern how many of those assets already belong to this new way of being Church. It is also my firm conviction that the gospel may be lost not just to a new generation but also to a new age that requires a vastly different way of being Church in order for the gospel to maintain its impact.

Glimpses of the Spirit

A final story as I close this chapter. I was invited to keynote at an annual banquet hosted by one of our largest and healthiest churches 2.0. They had heard me talk about church 3.0, and wanted me to come and speak about that with them.

That night was electric. These people, largely an elderly but vital, strong, and active congregation, were just really excited about what they were hearing. Part of that was my own energy, passion, and enthusiasm for the subject, but mostly it was their dawning awareness that the birthing of this new way of being Church might relieve their fears that the Church would die with them. They sensed that they had reason to believe that the gospel would be kept alive for their grandchildren.

When my presentation ended, there was time for some Q and A. The very first question that was asked was: "How do we become church 3.0?"

My response was simply: "You don't."

There was a collective gasp. They thought that is exactly what they had invited me to teach them.

We spent the rest of the time talking less about how to become church 3.0 than how to relate to church 3.0. I told them that they were everything church 2.0 was built to do and be at its best. I told them they had every reason to expect and believe they were going to be healthy and vital for a long time to come. I told them that if they tried to make a radical change, they would compromise that vitality and enter a market that they not only didn't understand but also couldn't excel at while others around them would. They would surely suffer as a result.

"So", I said, "continue to be the best church 2.0 you can be."

Then, as time was running low and the evening was coming to an end, there came one last question. "Can you come back and teach us what we need to do to support church 3.0?" I damn near did a dance right in front of them. I told them of course I would and, before I walked out the door, we had a date on the calendar to do just that. Three months later we would meet again for that conversation.

It was on that night that I knew the conversation we had been engaged in was one the entire Church needed to have. That's when the idea of this book came to me.

There is much to be said about how church 2.0 relates to church 3.0. I believe that a critical part of that relationship will have to do with whether or not the Church I serve can see the Church emerging as a covenant partner with whom it is called to share missional resources—not as gift, mind you, but as a wise and faithful stewarding of the missional resources with which we have been entrusted and believing that in doing so we safeguard those resources for the sake of the gospel.

CHAPTER THREE

Grieving, Believing, Perceiving

"Now, God be praised, that to believing souls gives light in darkness, comfort in despair."

- William Shakespeare

Churches aren't just called to die; they are also called to believe in resurrection and hope.

I am deeply indebted to David Ruhe for this title, and for much of the content of this chapter. David is a brilliant man and the devoted Senior Pastor at Plymouth UCC in Des Moines, Iowa.

I had the distinct honor of attending an event with him in Chicago, during which time we got to share some drinks and some deep conversation. I had known him and admired him for some time, but those days deepened my respect and appreciation for him. I would also discover his deep and abiding love for the Church.

It was April of 2012 and we were attending our annual United Church of Christ convocation. Each year in the early spring or late winter, national and conference leaders, seminary presidents, and board chairs are called together to address relevant matters regarding the life and future of our denomination. There were two things about the 2012 gathering that should be noted in setting this context. The first is that the Collegium of Officers had announced that they were going to unveil their strategies for living out the long-term goals for the denomination. The second was that, with so much at stake, "tall steeple pastors" (those who serve in large membership churches) were also invited. That's why David was there; his church in Des Moines is one of the largest in the denomination.

In the hours following the presentation by the collegium of their strategies for our future growth and vitality, I found myself in a room with David and about twenty or thirty others. The presentation had created quite a buzz, and people everywhere wanted an opportunity to talk about what we had heard. It was in that group that David shared with us what he had come to see as the most important work of the Church in this time.

When he finished, I was deeply moved. His words struck me immediately as profound and meaningful. I asked his permission to use them, knowing that I would have opportunity as a representative of the wider Church to speak in many settings where the words would be both appropriate and important. I crafted my presentation later that month to my conference annual meeting delegates around those insights. A few months after this, I was invited to one of my churches and sat and watched them play a tape of that presentation to their entire church. That's how moved they were by them. That's a testimony to how powerful these insights are to the work of the Church in our time.

David believes that the Church now has three critical tasks: grieving, believing, and perceiving. I will do my best in this chapter to get at exactly what I heard David say that afternoon in Chicago.

Grieving

I don't remember when I first heard someone talk about the Church living in a time of diminishment, or through a time of diminishing resources. I do remember thinking that it was an apt way of describing this time.

I also remember spending one of my many nights on the road sharing a hotel room with my dear friend Mike Denton, a Pacific Northwest Conference Minister. It was shortly after the collapse of the market—late 2008, or perhaps early 2009. As we always do at the end of our long days together, we were using the quiet time together in the room before we fell asleep talking about a variety of things. One of those things was the financial constraints we were all beginning to feel.

We noted that many leaders in the Church were taking a sort of "batten down the hatches, ride out the storm, and when things settle down take corrective measure" attitude toward the downturn in the economy. Mike then said something that I haven't forgotten, and that struck me as pure wisdom. He said, "John, this could be the new normal."

The new normal. This turn of phrase has stuck with me. In other words, the resources lost this time around may not be coming back. Strategic thinking about how to get them back may have to give way to strategic thinking about how to be the Church with less.

What does it mean to be the Church in a time of diminishing resources? We are all struggling with this and, as good leaders, we are doing everything we can to remind the Church that our vitality depends on our ability to be good stewards of the resources we have for the sake of the mission for which we were birthed.

Let there be no doubt that there have been, are, and will be, for some time to come, losses to sustain. I will talk about some of those, but before we get there. Let's also admit up front that most of those losses come with the experience of a real, and at times, profound grief. And so it is that, with the new normal in this time of diminishing resources, the first task of the Church is to grieve.

This is important. This is very important.

We live in the context of a culture that doesn't deal well with grief. I believe that is a byproduct of living in a world of rampant and unchecked consumerism. We are conditioned to anesthetize pain and grief and to invest in a panacea of market products that promise relief but which, in reality, only mask our underlying pain. That's another subject for another time. What I mean to suggest here is that we have been conditioned to either deny, repress, or medicate away our pain and grief. To do so in this time of diminishment, when the Church is going to sustain heavy losses, would be unhealthy.

A collective call to grieve can easily be met with fear and skepticism. It can be resisted both because of that condition we have inherited in our culture to repress grief and by those who are unwilling or unable to accept that the Church is living into a new normal and who believe we will soon, and somewhat miraculously I would argue, return to our halcyon days of sanctuaries filled to the brim and offering plates overflowing with riches.

As bearers of the light, however, and as disciples of Christ, we are reminded that we don't grieve as others who have no hope. We know that weeping may last for the night, but joy comes in the morning. It is ok to talk about this grief. It is imperative that we invite our leaders into a time of appropriate grief, knowing that grief will not be the last word spoken by the Church.

I'm going to pause here and acknowledge that, at this point, I have been writing mostly about the Church in decline, diminishment, and pain. The writing has produced my own need to process grief. I can well imagine that something like this can be happening to the reader as well. I will continue through this chapter to write about that diminishment.

Here's the thing—I am not sure we can adequately and properly grieve unless we name what it is that our eyes are seeing, our hearts are feeling, and our ears are hearing. There is profound loss all around us, and some of that loss is terribly hard for us to take. Collectively the sense of loss leaves some among us not only experiencing real pain and grief but also wondering how the Church can survive it and whether or not our lifetime commitment to it has been in vain.

I am talking about these losses with raw honesty. I admit freely to the grief I experience along the way. I do not grieve, however, as others who have no hope. I see with new eyes what the Spirit is doing in this time and the call I feel to write about all of this is not a call to talk about what is falling apart, but what is coming. In the end, this is not a word of despair but of deep and profound hope because of what I believe is emerging on the horizon. Hang in there with me, dear reader.

Some of this loss I have experienced in deeply personal ways. When I came on staff here in the Southwest Conference, we had some very talented, very dedicated men and women working for us. It took me a while to wrap my head around our finances, especially given that I arrived in late spring of 2008, about nine months before the market turned. It would take almost another two years to process how deeply that market turn would impact our budget and to accept that the money lost was probably not coming back.

At the same time this was happening, the Board of the Southwest Conference, with the help of some very gifted men and women who would form our Financial Advisory Task Force, made a covenant promise to present a balanced budget to our Annual Meeting delegates. We were able to do that by 2010. I will never forget what I now characterize as one of the most painful phone calls I have ever participated in.

It was October of 2009, and we knew that we had made the commitment to present a balanced budget. Annual Meeting would be in the spring of 2010. Throughout the year of 2009, we were hearing from churches who were telling us they could not complete their pledges to us. Tales of elderly members whose income was dependent on money drawn from their investments; of wage earners being laid off or downsized out of income; of homes being foreclosed on were shared with us by pastors telling us why they weren't going to meet their budget, and therefore were cutting their pledge to us.

Our budget was soundly built on those pledges from our churches and was passed with every reasonable expectation that we could live within it. By October, we knew we couldn't. We had to make some hard choices. One option was that we would not fulfill our covenant promise of balancing our budget. Who could argue that given the circumstances we did anything short of our best? Who would hold it against us if in fact under these circumstances we failed on our first attempt to balance our budget? There were some on the phone who argued we would be forgiven, and that we should just ride this out.

For others, though, a promise to our churches was not something we should treat lightly. We quickly gave ourselves over to the task of cutting what we could. The cuts were deep and painful. We lost our incredibly gifted and much loved Communication Director. We dropped the position of Youth and Outdoor Ministry Coordinator. Trips were cancelled. Promises were made by the remaining staff to work fewer hours—which only meant they worked the same hours but didn't charge the Conference for them.

The pain of that October 2009 phone call with my financial advisory team is something I still feel. It didn't end there. I had to follow up that phone call with meetings with our Board, asking them to approve the cuts we were recommending. I then had to meet with respective staff members, some of whom were told that they were losing their jobs. I had to stand before a delegation of representatives from all of our churches and report these losses. Acknowledging the diminishment was one source of grief. Losing the talent was another. But nothing compared to the grief of saying goodbye to people and losing the relationships that we had built with them over the years.

In May of 2010, I found myself working with five churches in my conference who reported to their pastors that they were cutting their salaries. For two of those five, the news was worse. It wasn't just that they were cutting salaries, they were eliminating the position of pastor altogether. Two of the remaining pastors were able to deal with the cuts, though it wasn't easy. The other pastor would work for a little over a year and half with the church to figure out how to care for her family with a salary that had been cut in half, a mortgage she was upside down in and couldn't get out of (meaning she couldn't think about moving and looking for another call), and how to meet the needs of the church working fewer hours.

One of those five churches not only dismissed the pastor, they shut down all operations. First Congregational United Church of Christ in Tucson had once been a strong, vital, relevant church. The closing of the church sent ripples of fear and grief throughout the Southwest Conference. While the service of closure was a beautiful testimony to the church's ability to regard its past with dignity and to engender hope in midst of profound loss, there is no doubt that real, deep, and abiding pain was palpable in that sanctuary. When I visit one of their sister churches now, I step into the narthex and see the stained glass window that hung in the entrance of First Church. I feel that sense of loss all over again.

These losses are painful, to be sure. For me, though, the most painful work I do today is with clergy. I don't know that I can capture all that they are experiencing in and through this time, but I will try. It is important for the Church to own what is happening to clergy.

I don't mean to suggest that these dynamics I describe are universal. They are not felt by all clergy everywhere but my experience is that they are far from uncommon. The first sense of loss that many clergy feel is simply a loss of job security.

One of my great joys as a Conference Minister is working with search committees. I spend a lot of time with them during the period of transition from retiring/resigning pastor, to interim pastor, to newly called pastor.

When I first started, I would include in my orientation with a search committee a review of their salary packages. I would explain to them that their profiles had to serve as a marketing tool for the church in what was a very competitive market. Part of the market strategy would not just be talking about what set their church apart, but stretching themselves enough so that their salary and benefits package would appeal to a prospective candidate. It was, as I told them, a "pastor's market."

I would explain that the Church was retiring more pastors than they were ordaining, and had been for some time. I would add that many of the clergy being ordained were second career people who would serve the Church not for 40-50 years, but for 15-20. Given these dynamics, there were more churches looking for pastors than there were pastors available. Pastors had choices, and were being smart with them.

All of that changed in 2009. All of a sudden, churches that had been stretched a bit to cover the expenses of a full-time pastor were finding it harder and harder to do that. Health care alone for a pastor and her family now approaches almost $20,000. As church members were losing jobs and income and church budgets were shrinking fast, more and more churches found that for the first time they were faced with the prospect of not being able to pay their pastor.

I noted that with almost every search committee with whom I worked, there was conversation in the time of transition about how to cut the budget for pastoral staff. If they were a large church with multiple pastoral staff positions, they had to use the interim time to talk about how the staff would be reconfigured in the time of transition. If they were a smaller church with a solo pastor, they talked about how to continue with less than a full-time pastor.

Five years ago, pastors were almost guaranteed a call when their profile circulated, but today it is not uncommon for very talented, very experienced pastors to be in search for more than two years.

I learned that in January of 2009, 125 pastors filed papers with the Pension Boards to retire and draw income from their pension. Only 25 of them actually went on to retire. Many of them had lost over half of their collected pension resources in the last quarter. Now, pastors aren't retiring nearly as quickly as they thought they might. They are delaying it for as long as they can, meaning that pulpits that, in previous years, would be open, aren't just yet.

Where five years ago I was telling search committees to be smart about how they competed for the pastors who were out there, today I have to talk to clergy about how to be willing to accept much less than what they had grown accustomed to in the past.

Today, I counsel all of our seminarians to think seriously about how they are going to earn an income while living out their vocation to the Church. I advise them that they should not take for granted that their income will come from the Church.

Every two years, all Conference staffs from across our denomination gather for a week at what used to be called our Search and Call training. It is now called AM21 (Authorizing Ministry for the 21st Century), but it is still a week long training to keep us up to date on the dynamics of staffing churches through their time of transition. In December of 2012, we gathered in New Orleans for the training. I attended a workshop called "Are We Deceiving Our Members in Discernment?" The entire discussion centered on whether this denomination was deceiving seminarians by asking them to go deep in debt without the promise of real income on the other side of ordination. It was, to say the least, a very lively conversation.

I cannot imagine having that conversation even two years prior. I now advise clergy not to even think about looking for another church if they are in one that is paying them a living wage with benefits.

There is an emerging sense of fear and anxiety experienced by men and women who have given their lives in service to the Church. They work endless hours for modest incomes. Until very recently, they have been reasonably hopeful that if they invested years in training, after acquiring a unique set of skills that would serve them and the Church well they would always be able to provide for their families. It is getting harder and harder for many of our pastors to look years down the road and have that assurance.

Many of our clergy are at an age when finding another source of comparable income is unlikely, given their narrow focus on developing skills sets unique to the Church. Some feel trapped. Some are living painfully with and through repeated cuts to budgets. This can mean frozen salaries without even cost of living raises in most years, deep cuts to their salaries and benefits packages, or (in the most extreme cases) the painful admission that the church just can't pay them anything any more and are cutting the position of pastor. Some with whom I have counseled are seriously contemplating filing for bankruptcy.

Two generations ago the Church noticed that after giving a lifetime in service to the Church, many pastors were ending their ministry without having had any income set aside for retirement. Mostly low wage earners serving in small churches in rural settings, these pastors faced 20 years or more of life left to live with no promise of steady income, and very little savings. Knowing that the church owed them more than this, the United Church of Christ established the Christmas Fund. Every year, every church in the denomination took up an offering to help these men and women.

Today, the Church faces a crisis of a very different kind. How is it going to face the crisis of pastors in their 40s, 50s, and 60s who lose their income from the Church and are not able to compete in a job market where even those who have been trained for and have experience in that market outside the church aren't getting hired? Clergy everywhere are experiencing, in very personal ways, what this time of diminishment means.

The grief and anxiety that clergy experience aren't entirely about loss of income. It isn't just about facing an uncertain financial future for both their churches and their families. The source of their grief is much deeper than that. I don't know that I can fully capture this, but it has a lot to do with feeling like a failure.

I want to be clear. No pastor I know is a failure. With very few exceptions, these are men and women of the highest quality and caliber. They have acted with deep conviction out of a strong sense of call. They are agents for change, for transformation, and for the common good. They do noble work daily, and very few notice. They make tremendous sacrifices to do what they do and rarely do I hear them complain about any of it.

There is great joy in ministry, and the rewards we are offered for it are not calculated merely by whatever financial compensation we receive. The joy comes in other ways. I remember after I did my first funeral, a moment for which I felt totally unprepared, the widow came back to church three weeks after her husband was buried. She met me outside my office, took my face in her hands, and with tears in her eyes said "I could never have gotten through this without you."

I remember walking down a hospital corridor and hearing the screams of a woman dying of a vicious cancer. When I walked into the room and she saw me, she suppressed the screams. I knew I wouldn't stay long, because I could see how much it was costing her to do that. I asked her if she would like to spend a moment in prayer and she nodded. I took her hand, closed my eyes for a quiet moment to center myself, and before I could say a word I heard her voice: "Dear God, please hold our pastor in your tender care and mercy. He means so much to us and is always there when we need him. Give him strength and let him know how much we love him. Amen."

To be engaged in ministry is to be called to be present at some of the most meaningful human experiences and to witness to God's grace in the midst of them. Over a lifetime of ministry, those experiences come to far outweigh whatever challenges might be sprinkled in during those years. As a judicatory officer of the Church, I often have the opportunity to sit and reflect with clergy who are coming to the end of their ministry. To hear them talk with pride, with joy, and with satisfaction about what their years in ministry have meant to them is a privilege I have come to cherish deeply.

Lately, though, I am hearing a very different refrain from these men and women. They have spent their latter years watching the churches they serve go into serious decline. This is not a universal experience. I can't say this is true of everyone. But so many pastors, good pastors, qualified pastors who for years have honed their craft with great care and attention, are experiencing the frustration of now putting those skills to use, but to no avail.

Meeting after meeting of their boards are consumed with repeated refrains about budget deficits, membership losses, and failed Sunday Schools and Youth programs. One of the standards by which we judge our tenure in ministry is whether or not we can say that when we leave, the Church is in better shape than when we got there. That is getting harder and harder for so many of us to say, in spite of our best efforts.

Clergy now face retirement and wonder what will be left behind them when they leave. Clergy look at their church's shrinking budgets and realize that but for their salaries, the church would be operating in the black. There is emerging in this context a frustration that comes from so much effort, so much skill being brought to bear with so little to show for it. There is emerging in this context a growing sense of despair that we can't stop it. There is emerging in this context a collective wonderment about failure on the part of so many. There is emerging in this context a sense among the retired clergy that they were wise to get out while they could. There is emerging in this context a collective sense of loss and with that a palpable sense of very real grief.

There is so much sadness in this. I see skilled, dedicated, passionate women and men working tirelessly, creatively, energetically, relentlessly and feeling like there is so little to show for it. Despite all their best efforts, budgets continue to shrink and membership rolls continue to decline. They worry now about their ability to provide for their family. Many feel like they have failed the Church, and for some of them—too many, really—their churches are more than happy to lay the blame at their feet. It is heartbreaking.

I am persuaded by David Ruhe's wisdom. The Church will be invited in these days to grieve deeply. That is not to say that we won't, at the same time, find plenty to celebrate. We will. That is also not to say that grief will be the end of our work together. It will not be.

The Church is experiencing real and profound loss: church closings; staff cuts; program cuts; untenable futures in once healthy and vital congregations; the absence in many settings of children and youth; clergy wondering from where the next call, if not the next paycheck, is going to come. There is much to grieve. We are called upon to own it. We are called upon to name it. We are called upon to endure it. We are called upon to experience it—but not as others do who have no hope. There is hope.

Believing

Which brings me to what David Ruhe sees as the Church's second task: believing. Because so much is changing, whether we like it or not, it is now incumbent on the leadership of the Church to think long and hard about what we believe. What are our non-negotiables? With so much on the table, including some very sacred cows, are there core values, accepted practices, or fundamental beliefs that, if these change, we cease to be? What losses, once sustained, signal the end?

These are important questions. It's not the first time the Church has faced this prospect of radical change. There have been critical moments in the life of the Church when new circumstances, new information, new dynamics have forced the question of change.

It is very important to adopt a relationship toward the new. For those who have been fed by current patterns, practices, and policies, decisions must be made about how to relate to what is emerging. If you opt for change, choosing what gets tossed aside and what gets held onto is critical. In her book *The Great Emergence How Christianity Is Changing and Why*, Phyllis Tickle refers to this as the Church's "great rummage sale."

When a household decides to have a rummage sale, they don't open the doors of their home to complete strangers and invite them to make an offer on anything they find in the house. Instead, they carefully, painstakingly evaluate which of their treasured possessions no longer serve the needs of the family. Often with some reluctance, those items are singled out and either sold or given away. There is never any question, though, that some items remain.

If, as Phyllis suggests, the Church is going through its 500-year rummage sale, then leaders in the Church are now called upon to make important and wise decisions about what stays and what goes. Some of this may well be done one church at a time, but not all of it. One church might get rid of their organ or their pews. One might even sell their property. That's different than the Church collectively debating the divinity of Jesus, the Trinity, the ordination of LGBT folk, and the need for, and role of, denominations.

Think about the early Jesus movement. Jesus was himself a Jew intent on reform. For his disciples, Jews themselves, he was an advocate and impetus for change. A quick read through Acts and some of Paul's letters reminds us that the first generation church was having their own "rummage sale." At the center of this reform movement known early on as "The Way" was a fierce and open debate about circumcision. Keep it or not?

Paul understood that this was larger than just a question of circumcision. At stake was this emerging movement's relationship to the law. His letter to the Galatians was a vitriolic, angry letter. In it, Paul bares his teeth: "You foolish Galatians? Who has bewitched you...? The only thing I want to learn from you is this: did you receive the Spirit by doing the works of the law or by believing what you heard? Are you so foolish...? For all who rely on the works of the law are under a curse!" (from his 3rd chapter)

Phyllis' metaphor may be a bit colloquial, but it works. In the rummage sale held by that first generation there were those who wanted to throw out both circumcision and the law as a means of acquiring right relationship with the creator.

James thought differently. When he learned that Peter baptized a Gentile before circumcising him (in Acts 10), James immediately assembled a council in Jerusalem. With the weight of his office and authority, James compelled Peter to come before the arbiters of orthodoxy and defend himself (Acts 11). Peter's words, and the influence of Paul on the early church, affected a significant change in the early church. This shift differentiated them from other Jewish sects that did not accept those changes. Circumcision became one of the items discarded by the early church in its rummage sale.

Phyllis Tickle observes that these rummage sales happen approximately every 500 years, which is why the Church is going through this upheaval now. Like that first generation church, there are circumstances forcing a shift in the Church, as we know it. Like that first generation of disciples, the Church as we know it is going to have to live through open debate about what changes can and will be accepted, and what changes simply cannot be made.

Be aware that every time a decision like this is made, there is the potential for a division of the body. Some will buy into the change. Others will live on with their firm conviction that the circumstances warrant an even stronger adherence to what grounds us.

There are going to be those whose orientation to the new will be resistance at all costs. There are going to be those whose orientation to the new will be acceptance. Either way, a call to be very clear about what you believe is essential. Knowing, through the time of change, what is so important that, if it is altered, we cease to be is an essential task of the Church. Knowing what must be passed on through the sea of change that is coming is important.

I have been doing an exercise with churches for the better part of the last decade. I ask them what their non-negotiables are. As you face your future, what can change, and what can't? Being prepared ahead of time for this will ground a church through the winds of change that are blowing. It is fascinating to watch them go through this exercise. There is intense debate along the way about what can go and what can't. Learning that there are deep emotional attachments to some things that others feel should go into the rummage sale makes for some very interesting conversation.

There are distinctions to be made between those precious things that we would grieve the loss of and those things that we absolutely cannot exist without. Many of us in the Church today are going to face a time of choosing between the one kind and the other. By what criteria will we be prepared to make these decisions?

Place yourself in Europe 500 years ago. The entire continent was awash not only with change but also with the kinds of decisions that often came with life or death consequences. In the rummage sale that was the Reformation, individuals, congregations, towns, cities, and nations faced choice with very real consequences.

In the decades preceding the Reformation, a monk in England by the name of John Wycliffe translated the Bible into English. For the Orthodox Church, this was a non-negotiable. After his death, the church declared him a heretic and had his body exhumed and burned. One of his disciples, Jan Hus, had to make a similar a decision. Like Wycliffe, he was a monk who, in Prague, began teaching about the new way to be the church that included translating the Bible into the vernacular. When he did just that, he was burned at the stake.

This went on throughout the entire European continent. Princes fought wars over commitments to the old way or the new way. Individual leaders, both lay and clergy, throughout the continent brought congregations with them one way or the other. Over the next two centuries, the Reformation would take hold, but not without a lot of bloodshed.

I don't foresee executions and burnings this time around, but the same moment is going to confront many of us. How much of what is going to change can we tolerate before we say enough? And what lines will we draw that direct us to one side or the other?

Some of us have already faced these moments.

Will we ordain somebody who hasn't completed seminary?

Will we accept as authentic baptisms that are being performed by those with no authorization from the Church?

Will we ordain a candidate who says she doesn't believe Jesus is the son of God?

Will we ordain openly LGBTQ men and women?

Can we allow a church to elect a non-baptized, practicing Jew who is not a member of their church to serve as the President of their congregation?

Can we accept into membership of our church someone who has not been baptized and doesn't want to be?

Will we affiliate a church whose spiritual leader is not an authorized, trained clergy person and who places a Buddha next to the font during baptisms?

Not one of these is a hypothetical situation. Every single one of the questions is one I have watched church leaders wrestle with. I have sat with the Church as it has engaged in open deliberation with every single one of these questions, and many more besides.

On what grounds, basis, or foundation are decisions like these made? Who has the right to speak for the whole when confronted with questions like these? At what point does it become clear that resolving any of these questions in either the affirmative or the negative creates a line of demarcation that some can cross, others cannot? When does a new divide emerge that substantively separates what has been from what will be?

It is going to take a century or more, I am told, for this to shake out and for us to know whether or not something new is emerging. Only then will we know exactly what it is. Only then will we know exactly how it relates to what has been. Only then will we know what it was that made the distinction necessary.

In the meantime, the Church is compelled to get very clear about what it believes. The Church is compelled to distinguish between how much of what they currently believe is a byproduct of culture, gender, orientation, etc. How much of what they currently believe cannot be sacrificed on the altar of change?

I don't imagine that there will be anything close to uniformity or unanimity in the resolution of these grand questions that the Church is facing. There will be a multiplicity of voices vying for attention, claiming with varying degrees of voracity what is appropriate and what is not.

Regardless, I can't imagine leadership in the Church being relevant today without extending a call to all partners to engage in open dialogue about what matters most. I also can't imagine being a leader without speaking with some clarity about what matters most to me and why.

Perceiving

Which brings us to the third calling of the Church in this time: perceiving. Paul does remind us that we don't experience loss the same way as others do who have no hope. Grief brings with it a real and often residual pain. We have come to know, however, that whatever weeping we do in the night is replaced by a joy that comes in the morning.

As Jesus once said, let those who have eyes to see, see. This is about perception.

Who among us has the vision to see beyond the time of grief, beyond the horizons of pain to what lies on the other side? This is about perceiving.

This is about seeing through the tears and the weight of our collective grief so that we not be overcome by a despair that blinds us to the hope that awaits.

I believe it is time for the shamans among us to find their voice. I believe it is time for spiritual guides and directors to emerge and with their poetry, their dance, their art, their music, their tongue entice us to those places where the Spirit is living, breathing, and calling us to new embraces of wonder, imagination, creativity, and— dare I say it—hope.

There are among us, as there have always been throughout the life of the Church, those who are especially sensitive to the movement and impulse of God's Holy Spirit. With a sensitivity that rational thought cannot explain or defend, these women and men experience profound insights that get communicated through poetry, art, dance, music, parable, narrative. They have always lived and walked among us but they have not always been honored.

Living through the time of the Enlightenment, which the Reformation Church did, we could not help but be influenced by a western culture that came to rely almost exclusively on deductive reasoning, scientific proof, and the deep intellect as tools used to test what is real and what is not. We put those tools to good use and, in the process, discovered much that changed our way of thinking, of living, and of perceiving who we are and how we walk in this world.

Western culture since the time of the Enlightenment has placed a high value on objective, rational, deductive reasoning. It calls upon independent bodies to serve without bias in the testing of, and eventual establishment of, what we accept as good, truthful, and enduring. It sees personal opinion, personal experience, personal thought, emotion, and temperament to be impediments to truth that must be avoided at all costs. The testing of postulated theorems must include an ability to demonstrate the lack of bias, emotion, and mere perception.

Essential to this way of thinking and perceiving the world is the maintenance of a dichotomy between mind and body, flesh and spirit, material and spiritual. Those of us who have been raised to practice the spiritual arts have come to see the flesh as an impediment to our higher spiritual goals. It is that which makes us weak when face to face with temptation. Those who walk in the scientific world see the ineffable as an impediment to what the material world requires in the way of evidence. We can't let emotions like joy, anger, fear, hope, or anxiety impede our ability to analyze the data before us.

Through all of this, the Church has often failed to identify those who have been blessed with the charism of spiritual discernment. The Church itself has not been immune from the tendency to reduce our truth to that which we can measure, test, and subject to rational thought. It is not that we have lost the art of spiritual discernment and the truth that comes from inductive reasoning and intuition. We have simply, more often than not, disregarded it.

It is time to call forth those who practice this art, and whose gift is discernment. We need to invite them to find their voice. We need them to remind us that we too can see the world with new eyes. We need to ask them what they see, so that our own perceptions are altered. We need to give them permission and latitude to express their vision in whatever artful language is most accessible to them. We need to develop our own ability to intuit. We need to give ourselves permission at times to trust impulse and instinct against reason. We need to cultivate the ability to perceive that which is hidden to the rational mind. We need to let the subtle, the ineffable, and the mysterious remind us again of all that awe and wonder are able to do.

There is much more to see in front of us than a dying church. There is more to perceive than the diminishment of resources. There is more to experience than grief. It is time not just to hope against hope, but to discover what there is beyond the horizon of our grief that grounds us in hope. And that is about perception.

In his book *The Prophetic Imagination*, which I read more than twenty-five years ago and so won't get this exactly right, Walter Brueggemann writes about the daring vision of the prophet. The prophet has an ability to imagine what others could not.

When the Kings were in power, and with that power started amassing a wealth that blinded them to the plight of the poor among them, it was the prophets who imagined a time of pending ruination that the Kings could not see. Listen to Amos: "Hear this word, you cows of Bashan who are on Mount Samaria, who oppress the poor, who crush the needy, who say to their husbands, 'Bring me something to drink!' The Lord has surely sworn by the Lord's holiness: The time is surely coming upon you, when they will take you away with hooks, even the last of you with fishhooks." (Amos 4:1-2) It was hard to believe that such a circumstance was possible.

When the exiles were sent into the wilderness with nothing and were sure that God had abandoned them, the prophets imagined a day of reconciliation and hope they simply could not see. We hear this in the words of Second Isaiah: "Comfort, O comfort my people, says your God. Speak tenderly to Jerusalem, and cry to her that she has served her term, that her penalty is paid, that she has received from the Lord's hand double for all her sins." (Isaiah 40:1-2)

Amos spoke to the wealthy who could not imagine anything but that God would continue to reward them with wealth and power. Isaiah spoke to exiles who could not imagine that God would ever love or forgive them again. This is the prophetic imagination. This is about seeing with new eyes what God intends. This is about perception.

Let those who have eyes to see, see. Let them speak the vision. Tell them to make it plain. "Write the vision; make it plain on tablets, so that a runner may read it. For there is still a vision for the appointed time. It speaks of the end, it does not lie. If it tarries, wait for it; it will surely come, it will not delay." (Hab 2.2-3)

There is no denying that part of what is fueling our grief is the pace of change. We can't keep up. We are overwhelmed. What worked so well for us not that long ago isn't working anymore.

Even those of us who are open to change aren't sure we can tolerate this much change.

For those among us who can only see grief ahead, we listen for the voices of those with prophetic imagination. We invite them to share with us what it is they see in the future. We pray for the courage and the conviction to perceive with new eyes what lies beyond the horizon of our grief. This, too, shall pass. Perceiving does not arrive so that we can hide from our grief; but it does persist so that we do not face grief as others who have no hope. In a time of great change and tumultuous transformation, when the pain of loss and uncertainly are all too real, new perceptions will emerge and ground us in an abiding hope.

Grieve, Believe, Perceive

I once heard Michael Kinnamon deliver a keynote address titled "It's a Great Time to Be the Church." He was addressing everything that we are talking about here: diminishment, rapid and uncontrollable change, grief, abandonment by the youth and young adults, etc. His ability to trust the movement of the Spirit and to see hope on the horizon has been a lingering source of inspiration to me.

I agree with him. It is a great time to be the Church. There is hard and painful work ahead. I have no doubt that in time the Church will look back on this moment and be grateful both for those who had the courage to change, and those who had the courage to hold strong to their convictions. I have no doubt, for some, both will be required.

Grieving, believing, perceiving: three tasks to which the Church is called in this time of dramatic change. These are not easy tasks, but these are also not easy times. It is not for the faint of heart. If you are a person of faith engaged in the life of the Church today, you have undoubtedly already experienced some grief. You will be invited either in the midst, or in the aftermath, of that grief to see things with new eyes. You will also be encouraged to clarify what it is you are willing to accept with those new eyes and what you simply cannot.

It really is a great time to be the Church!

CHAPTER FOUR

2.0 and 3.0

"God writes the gospel not in the Bible alone, but on trees and flowers and clouds and stars."

- Martin Luther

Every model needs an upgrade, but sometimes you just need to start over.

It was Cameron Trimble who introduced me to this concept. For me, it serves as a shorthand way of talking about the paradigm shift we are living through. It is based on a somewhat oversimplified view of church history, but it serves its purpose.

It asks us to look at the Church as we have known it having developed through three eras: the Church before the Reformation, the Church after the Reformation, and the Church that some are saying is emerging in our time. As I said, it's an oversimplification.

With this use of shorthand, we can now refer to the Church before the Reformation as church 1.0, the Church after the reformation as church 2.0, and whatever is emerging as Church 3.0. The point being made in these classifications is simply this: with each of these manifestations of the Church, something fundamental shifted, something very basic. What happened wasn't just a tweaking of what came before. The change was such that those who initiated it came to an agreement with those who refused to accept it that something was fundamentally different. A whole new way of doing things is being proposed. When that new way is clearly identified, the world will forever distinguish what was and what will be.

It should be noted that when the Reformation came and a new way of being Church emerged, the old way of being Church did not disappear. There were, and remain to this day, adherents to that model. Church 1.0 is still alive and well. I see no reason to doubt that church 2.0 as we know it will succeed through whatever time of transition it might be living through right now.

It should also be noted that the Reformation changed the Roman church. It, too, went through its own reformation and would not be the same. I do not doubt that what is happening to the church today will effect long-lasting and meaningful changes on church

2.0 as well. As it grows through those changes, however, it will not cease to exist. What it offers will serve for quite some time as a viable option for many. I am persuaded that a third option is already present, though not yet clearly defined or established, that will enter the marketplace and give people of faith a fundamentally different choice: church 3.0.

I have already admitted that this shorthand way of describing a very large and complex church history is grossly oversimplified. It is by no means a comprehensive, adequate way of addressing this amazingly complex development in the life of the Church. I want to describe what I think are some of the fundamental changes that took place to distinguish church 1.0 from church 2.0, and then what will distinguish church 2.0 from church 3.0. As I do this, please know that the descriptions are also inadequate and a bit oversimplified. I admit that from the start.

Disclaimers

Before I do that, a few disclaimers. I am not a church historian. I am a practitioner of the faith with a good educational background and now more than twenty-five years of experience in service to the Church. I cannot, however, claim any level of expertise in this particular area. These will be broad strokes that I use here. I draw on what I have learned and read from others who have spent a great deal more time researching these matters. I have done a little of my own research. I do draw on personal relationships with leaders in church 3.0. I have taken the initiative not just to read about what they are doing but to be present with them in conversation as they live out their faith and their vision for what the Church might become.

Because I will paint these respective eras with broad strokes, fine details will be absent. I am looking at foundational and fundamental elements that define a given era. I am wondering what shifted and why, and observing that those shifts amounted to more than a modification of what had come before. Something substantively different was introduced that both the new and the old agreed would require a recognizable and established distinction between them.

When church 2.0 began reading the Bible in the vernacular, church 1.0 was happy to be distinguished from them. When church 2.0 went from seven sacraments to two and taught that Jesus was only symbolically present in the celebration of the Eucharist, church 1.0 had no problem with drawing lines of distinction between themselves and church 2.0.

We are only at the onset of church 3.0. That means I will be attempting to describe it not only with broad strokes, but also without the benefit of centuries of hindsight. No one can say much about it with a great deal of confidence. I am aware that while I suggest that there is already a demarcation that distinguishes church 2.0 from church 3.0, I cannot yet fully and satisfactorily say just what church 3.0 is. I do, however, begin with some underlying assumptions.

Assumptions

The first is that in fact this isn't just an adjustment. It is a demarcation between one way of being Church and a totally different way of being Church. I don't believe that the question being asked by church 3.0 is what can we do to make church 2.0 palatable for us. I argue that what is emerging not only cannot be absorbed into the model that is church 2.0, it should not be. The position I am taking is that this is something completely new and different that must be seen as distinct, in fact as distinct as we now see church 2.0 being from church 1.0.

I know many who feel that the best way to save church 2.0 from extinction is to co-opt church 3.0. Many believe that church 2.0 might need a little tweaking but, by and large, it is a structure worth preserving. It has served the Church very well for all these years. If 2.0 can make some necessary adjustments, there will be no need for anyone to abandon it. If church 2.0 can borrow the best minds church 3.0 has to offer and can benefit from some of their most creative thinkers, then necessary adjustments can be made and church 2.0 can be saved.

I am not in that camp. I am not saying that church 2.0 can't be saved. I don't think in those terms at all. As I say, I think church 2.0 is going to be around for a long time. I think that it, too, will go through some changes. It already has.

What I am saying here is that church 3.0 is an emerging option for people of faith. If it gets co-opted by church 2.0 because of a need it has to "save" itself, then the people of faith lose a very important and absolutely necessary third option. We enter postmodernity without a viable option for postmodern thinkers who have already left the Church.

I have seen this very thing tried, this effort for church 2.0 to adopt what they like about what church 3.0 is doing. It is my strong bias that not only does this not work, but it takes those creative postmodern minds and reduces their best and most innovative work to what church 2.0 can tolerate. To borrow more biblical language, it is putting new wine into old wine skins. I believe strongly that the Holy Spirit is behind this work, and that we should trust it. I believe that because the world has shifted so dramatically, the Spirit is birthing a new way of being Church so that the gospel message can be heard, received, and transmitted in ways the postmodern world can accept.

The second assumption I make is that not only is there already a distinction between a way of being church 2.0 and church 3.0, what is emerging isn't just a fad that will come and go. It will, in fact, survive its birthing stage and be written about as a distinct model another 300 years into the future. Of course we can't know that. I admit that up front. I am, however, accepting that as a given and will write from that perspective.

That has less to do with my confidence in the creative minds who are leading this movement. I do have confidence in them; don't get me wrong. I do place more confidence, though, in two other things that I think carry more weight here. The first is that postmodernity will require something new to sustain the faith. The second is that the Holy Spirit is behind this. Whatever gifts I have in my somewhat unpracticed art of discernment lead me to believe that at a pretty deep level.

Having made those disclaimers, I now go backwards in time and ask what happened 500 years ago and why. What compelled the Church to reform itself in such a way that history now distinguishes what came before, and what came after Luther tacked his 95 theses on the doors of the Wittenberg Cathedral?

Sola Scriptura

So said Luther. "By scripture alone" became the rallying cry of the early Reformers. That single notion compelled men and women across the European continent in the early sixteenth century to reform the Church.

There is a lot of history packed into those two Latin words. I will do my best to unpack some of that history and place that phrase in a context that will help us understand its import and impact.

It is the accepted teaching of the Roman church (what I have been referring to as church 1.0) that when Jesus gave Simon the name Peter ("the rock"), and later said "Upon this rock I will build my church," apostolic and papal authority were established. For the Roman church, apostolic authority derives its legitimacy from Peter himself. The laying on of hands descends across time and place from the pope himself, to and through the bishops, and finally to the priests. It is more than a symbolic representation of the hierarchy and authority vested in those upon whom hands have been laid. It is an actualization and perpetuation of a legitimacy established with, and perpetuated through time and space by, Peter.

For church 1.0, the tradition established by those with that actualized authority carries as much, if not more, weight as scripture. Over time, the doctrine of infallibility would be attached to Papal authority. All ordained clergy would take a vow of obedience, subjecting them to the will of those who ruled over them in the chain of hierarchy. For church 1.0, there were three pillars of orthodoxy: sacred scripture, sacred tradition, and *sacred magisterium*. When the pope spoke on matters of faith *ex cathedra* (literally "from the chair"), the *magisterium* of the Church was invoked and his words came to be accepted without error. The authority for that infallibility derives directly from the Christ's naming of Peter as his own authority on earth: "What you bind on earth shall be bound in heaven; what you loose on earth shall be loosed in heaven." (Matthew 16:18-19)

Fast forward to the time of the Middle Ages. Three things would conspire to help fuel a movement that would birth church 2.0. They were the schism of the papacy, the Black Death, and the invention of the printing press.

In 1378, Pope Gregory XI died. He would be the last of the Avignon popes, that is popes who resided in the city of Avignon in France. Upset that for 70 years the popes had been French, a group of cardinals called for a return to a Roman pope and elected Urban VI. The French faction refused to recognize his legitimacy, and elected Clement VII. When they died respectively, the same factions simply elected their own new pope to replace him until, in 1409, a third faction emerged who wanted a middle ground and elected Alexander V—a now third pope.

If you are a simple peasant in the European Middle Ages, your faith is a simple one. You accept what you are told by more educated people and you pay them proper respect. If, as has been the accepted order of the faith for over a millennium now, you are told that the Church derives its teachings from a pope, you have no trouble accepting that. Having believed that for so long now, one day you realize that there are three popes. This is unfathomable. It gives you pause. It shakes the foundation of a church built upon the principle that the pope is God's chosen representative on earth. You don't know or care much about the political machinations and subtleties and alliances that caused this new condition—you just feel lied to, and wonder how legitimate the whole affair can be if this essential ingredient is now missing.

So, three popes began to erode confidence in a pillar of church 1.0's foundation: *sacred magisterium*. And since sacred tradition, a second of those three pillars, was fundamentally derived from the *magisterium*'s authority, it would not be hard for reformers to begin to poke holes in that argument as well—leaving only one of the three pillars.

Attacks on the sacred tradition would soon also come. The primary source of this attack had to do with the practice of indulgences. Indulgences were opportunities offered by the church to relieve or reduce temporal punishment, which was required as an act of contrition for sins committed and confessed.

In theory, an indulgence can be the offering of a favorite prayer or an act of kindness, compassion, or love (among other things), but it became the practice of many in the church of the Middle Ages to assign a monetary value to indulgences. The abuse of this practice not only riled up the masses of very poor people across the continent, it eroded their confidence in the church's leaders. They came across to them as simply greedy. It began to feel to them like the indulgence was less about the amelioration of suffering for the living and the dead than it was a means of acquiring wealth by the church.

When reformers would come along and start talking about grace being offered unconditionally on the cross, therefore eliminating the need for an act of confession to a priest who would also coerce an indulgence from you, there were many who were willing to accept that teaching, whether in principle or just to relieve the stress on their household income. The argument found a ready and willing audience.

Add to this the fact that the Black Death was devastating much of Europe. Opportunities were ripe for corrupt church leaders to exact an even greater toll on the grieving poor. Those corrupt leaders used the plague as a way of shaming the living into more and more indulgences to relieve the suffering of the departed loved ones.

Now three popes and a poverty-stricken continent grown weary of the greedy corruption of many within the church made the elevation of the third pillar a likely candidate for a call to reform. Goodbye *sacred magisterium*. Goodbye sacred tradition. What was left? *Sola scriptura*—only scripture.

That the historical circumstances made Europe ready for reformation cannot be denied. Without a good delivery system, however, it is hard to imagine it succeeding. That's where Gutenberg comes in. His printing press revolutionized the world and became the fuel that made reform in the Church possible.

With the dawn of the printing press, dissemination of the Bible was made possible on a much broader scale. The book was translated into common languages of all peoples. Luther was among the most prominent church scholars of his time to argue for the centrality of scripture, and he did it at a time when scripture could be brought to the people. He was far from alone. Given the milieu in Europe, he found a continent ready to free itself from the corruption of the mother church. church 2.0 was ready to be birthed.

Phyllis Tickle writes that every generation seeks answers to deep, hard questions about the meaning of life and our place in the world. Because so much is at stake in this, every culture must establish some reliable source of authority that can be accepted to help distinguish between answers that are absurd and answers that are meaningful. For church 1.0, the *magisterium* of the church and the tradition it established and preserve through time served that very purpose. When disputes arose on the greatest questions faced by the world, the mother church through the papacy was there to arbitrate and resolve these conflicts. A way of being Church was constructed, built on the establishment of that authority.

Because of the papal schism, because of the abuse of indulgences in a time of massive plague and death, and because reformers were able to make good use of Gutenberg's printing press to circulate the Bible in mass quantities to poor peasants who had never had access to it before, the old way of being Church would no longer be seen by the world as their only option. Truth could no longer be subjected with any real credibility to a pope, and the church that built itself on that assumption became, for many people, a non-option.

The Reformation Church abandoned reliance on tradition and the *magisterium*. *Sola scriptura* became its rallying cry. From this point forward, both tradition and authority would be subjected to what scripture could and could not tolerate.

Because of that reliance on scripture, another very important shift took place for the church 2.0. This may seem like a subtle shift, but it had a deep and profound impact on the meaning, mission, and purpose of the Church. That was Luther's claim that we are saved by grace. Faith alone, not works, is redemptive.

This teaching of the Reformation Church diminished the role of the priest as an essential middle-man in the peaceful negotiation between penitent and God. Jesus' act of willing submission on the cross was sufficient to redeem us. Indulgences were no longer necessary. Confession as a sacrament and as a means of attaining forgiveness was no longer necessary. The priest was no longer the *sine qua non* in the process of reconciliation, forgiveness, and the dispensation of grace.

Sin was still an obstacle to be overcome, and the Church would have to play a role in overcoming its impact. church 2.0, however, would abandon the practice of confession and absolution through the hands of God's mediator, the priest. It would, instead, rely on both good preaching by educated clergy to touch the hearts and minds of the believers, and personal piety, confession, and good will on the part of the laity. Church 2.0 did not need anyone to mediate their relationship with God. church 2.0 completely changed its understanding of the role of the ordained.

What now divided church 1.0 from church 2.0 wasn't just theology. It was a radically new understanding of the role and purpose of the Church derived from fundamentally different understandings of from where the Church derived its authority.

Prior to the Reformation, church 1.0 was very clear that those questions would ultimately be settled by the pope. When speaking *ex cathedra*, he spoke as with the voice of God.

As we have already noted, that whole system falls apart in the eyes of the adherents when three different men claim to be the one to have that authority. In its stead, church 2.0 postulated that the Bible would serve as that authority: *sola scriptura*. A whole new way of being Church had to evolve because a whole new seat of authority was to be established.

As a result, clergy no longer served the role as dispensers of God's grace to a sinful world needing to be ritually purified through the sacrament of confession. Clergy, instead, would dedicate themselves to a lifelong pursuit of understanding and proclaiming scripture—

which now would be accessible to everyone—and that faithful proclamation would engender the creation and maintenance of *shalom*, a community of people living in good and right relationship with each other and with their creator.

In order to accept that there is, will be, and ought to be a church 3.0, there has to be an understanding that something as dramatically different is emerging in our world and our culture. Our current way of being Church will not hold. If the seat of authority that held church 1.0 together was no longer acceptable to many because of what was unfolding in the world around them, then for there to be a church 3.0 there would have to be a recognition that what held church 2.0 together is likewise no longer seen as valid.

Sola scriptura. It was an important insight for its time. As a foundational principle for birthing a new movement, it held together well for quite some time. For much of the Church today, it does so no longer. We can say a lot about church 3.0. Many have studied it deeply and thoroughly. At this point, I really only want to say one thing about it. For the postmodern mind, and therefore for church 3.0, *sola scriptura* as the only authority through which truth can be mediated just doesn't work any longer.

The Reformation Church had to be birthed when the *magisterium* could no longer serve as arbiter of and authority for truth. For the same reason church 3.0 is needed today. A church built upon a fundamental reliance on *sola scriptura* as the arbiter of truth, as the standard against which all truth must submit itself, and the lens through which all truth must be filtered, quite simply cannot be sustained in the postmodern mind. Loren Mead sensed this already in 1991 when he wrote his book *The Once and Future Church*, in which he argued that the changes coming would be as deep and meaningful to the Church as we know it as the Reformation had been before.

A New Foundation

When the foundation upon which an existing model of being Church no longer holds, a whole new foundation must emerge. I think that what is happening in the Church today is a struggle within a culture that no longer accepts the Bible as the primary source of our truth. Our reliance through the time of the Enlightenment on scientific research and development as well as the use of those tools to develop a far more sophisticated and

71

nuanced understanding of just what the Bible is and is not have eroded our confidence in *sola scriptura.*

What postmodern mind believes what the Bible has to say about homosexuality? About slavery? About the role of women in the Church, the culture, and the family? How many awkward sermons do preachers have to deliver on the sacrifice of Isaac, on Jesus calling the Syro-Phoenician woman a dog, or on Joshua being told to enter towns and slaughter all the men, women, children, and livestock in the name of God? Who is going to submit the limits of their belief structure and morality to a Levitical and Deuteronomic code that asks us not to wear shirts woven from two fabrics and to stone a woman raped inside the gates of the city who fails to cry out for help?

To be sure, sacred texts will continue to play a necessary and important role in the life of the Church and for people of faith. Fewer and fewer people, however, will make the claim that truth as we know and accept it must first be subjected to what the Bible can tolerate. This means, as painful as it is to write this, a church birthed in the cauldron of the Middle Ages in Europe as a reaction to the corruption of the *sacred magisterium* and founded on the claim that only scripture would and could authorize truth must now give way to a church looking to build its future on another foundation.

Welcome to church 3.0. Upon what will its foundation be built? We don't yet know. We have clues—but we don't know. It is a church in process. It could take the next 100 years for that to be fully understood.

I heard Phyllis Tickle answer this very question. What she said made my heart sing. It resonated very deeply with what I have been arguing for years. When asked what the foundation of this new way of being Church might be, she confessed she didn't know but, if forced to answer, would guess the Holy Spirit.

Whether that is true is yet to be discovered. I have no doubt that church 3.0 is emerging and is being blessed and inaugurated by God's Holy Spirit. The world has again shifted a bit on its epistemological axis. The vessel built to sustain the missional life of the Church will not sail easily in these new waters. Because the mission is far too important to compromise, the Spirit will do what is needed in order for the Church to remain meaningful and relevant. If that means the birthing of a new way of being Church, then so be it.

I want to end this chapter with one more thought. This can get really close to sounding like one way of being Church is good and another isn't. I don't believe that at all. What I do believe is that whether you choose church 1.0, church 2.0 or church 3.0 doesn't really make any difference as far as I am concerned. If any one of those models makes it possible for you to have a meaningful relationship with your creator and your neighbor and makes it possible for you to love yourself and be happy, then the Church as you know it is doing its job. I bear witness to the fact that in every model of the Church lives are changed and the common good is served. I live with the firm conviction that the Holy Spirit is alive and well wherever two or more gather and, in the gathering, covenant with each other to live a life of faithful commitment to one another, to neighbor, and to God.

What I do not any longer accept is a commitment to my way of being Church as the only legitimate and acceptable way because it works for me. If the call to be the Church must now be more fully lived out by shifting the paradigm, I consider that a blessing.

Given that, I think that whether you are a proponent and practitioner of church 1.0, church 2.0 or church 3.0, then be it fully and faithfully. Be that Church to the best of your ability. Do so knowing that there are many who have not yet heard of the redeeming and transformative love of God, and your invitation to them to experience that love will change their lives. Do so knowing that you have allies in this grand missional effort. No matter which expression of the Church you find most fulfilling, the other expressions are not your enemies. They pose no threat to you.

Remember this: Jesus reformed the Church, as he knew it. He was seen as a threat to an institution that already existed and to those who were authorized to serve with power inside that structure. Every time we live through these changes, that dynamic plays out.

Acts records an important deliberation between the power brokers of that church's existing structure. Peter and some of the other disciples had been imprisoned for their radical preaching. The Sanhedrin met. Voices emerged that called for them to be put to death. A lone voice stood among them and told them to reconsider. His name is given to us: Gamaliel. His words to the established orthodoxy of the existing religious authority of his time have been recorded for us: "in the present case I advise you: Leave these men alone! Let them go! For if their purpose or activity is of human origin, it will fail. But if it is from God, you will not be able to stop these men; you will only find yourselves fighting against God." (Acts 5:38-39)

I can think of no wiser words to share to the established authority of our time. I don't hear anyone asking to put people to death, but in the grief and anxiety, many of us are experiencing a growing need to

73

look with disdain at the church 3.0, to see them as a threat to us, and to wish that this passing fad would just hurry up and fade away.

If I had only one thing to say to church 2.0, a church I know and love, it would be this: "leave those people alone! Let them be (literally, not just leave them alone, but let them BE). For if their purpose or activity is of human origin, it will fail. If it is from God, you will not be able to stop it; you will only find yourselves fighting against God."

God's love endures. You exist in the Church and as the Church. You are faithful adherents to that fundamental belief. You have experienced the tremendous power of that transformative love yourself. You care enough about your neighbors, known and unknown, that you are willing to offer that love to them.

Nothing else matters. Whether 1.0 or 2.0 or 3.0, we are all in this together. Some will fall in love with God by coming to know her through the *magisterium* of the church. Some will fall in love with God by coming to know her through the living word. Some will fall in love with God by coming to know her by some other pathway.

It's all good.

CHAPTER FIVE

Postmodernity and Authority

"I strive to be kind: but not because I was told to."

- Laurie Seidler

There are two sides to the same coin we know as authorized, professional clergy: authority and authorization.

Authority in Ministry

On the first side of that coin, authority, there is a presumption that a trained professional who has been prepared and examined is granted permission to speak and act on behalf of the Church. Any church that extends a call to this professional will give her a venue in which, on matters of faith and spirituality, she will be expected to serve as an authority. In some of our faith traditions, she will be the sole arbiter of matters ecclesiastical and spiritual. In other traditions, she will be one among many. Even here, though, it will be conceded that her power will often trump all others. This is what authority means. She will speak with the weight of the Church at her disposal. For some, she will speak as with the voice of God. Pastors are given this kind of authority.

I remember two very cute stories from the time I was serving as a pastor in my first church. Little Timmy Wright was born just a few months before I moved from seminary to begin my ministry in Mayview, MO. When he was about three years old, he was sitting in church one Sunday morning next to his mother. The way the sanctuary was built, the pastor's chair was placed directly behind the pulpit. When I was sitting there, I was hidden by it. After my sermon that morning, as the offering was being collected, I sat in that chair to listen to the music being played by our organist. That's when Timmy looked up and saw that I had disappeared. He turned to his mom, looked up at her, and asked, "Mom, where did God go?"

Cute story number two is similar. Phillip Wagner was born a few years into my ministry at Mayview. He was adorable. My second son, Adam, was two years old when we moved there. By the time Timmy was born, Adam has outgrown his very first Cardinal baseball hat. Because this church was about 40 miles east of Kansas City, most of the members were KC Royals fans. We had a running feud going through my eight years there about that. I was a die-hard Cardinal fan. Because of that running feud, rather than just get rid of the hat that Adam had outgrown, one morning I gave the hat to little Timmy. Two weeks later, his mom came up to me and said with some irritation in her voice: "I wish to God you had never given him that stupid hat." I smiled, thinking that this was her way of keeping the feud going. She was upset that my plot to turn him into a Cardinal fan was working. Turns out, it wasn't that at all. She went on to say, "When he takes a bath, when he sits down to eat, when he goes to bed I tell him the same thing: 'Timmy, you have to take that hat off now.' He won't. I try to take it off, and he just insists on putting it back on his head. He refuses to ever take it off. When I asked him why, he just looked at me and said, 'Mommy, Jesus gave this to me.'"

I need to tell one more story while I'm making this point about authority. It's not a cute story. It's terribly sad. Lori was a twenty-four-year-old bride who was deeply in love with her husband. He was thirty-two. She and her family were pillars of that church in Mayview. Her smile was infectious, and never left her face. She was just a delight to be around. She and her husband had just moved into their new dream home. Life was good—very good.

I went to this church right out of seminary. It was a small church in a small town. Mayview's population was around 260 people. It was ten miles from a gallon of gas and a loaf of bread. I went my first year without a member of the church dying, so I hadn't yet done my first funeral when, a little past my first anniversary at the church, the phone rang. It was a Saturday morning and my wife was at work. She was a nurse.

I was at home working on my sermon and watching our three young children. I picked up the phone and heard a woman asking me if I was Pastor John. I said yes. She told me that a member of my church had just died. His wife was here at the hospital. She was hysterical and could not be calmed down. Could I come and help? I told her of course I would and asked who it was. She told me she didn't know. The man who had died had no ID on him and they had been trying for some time to calm her down and get some information from her, but couldn't. I said I would be there right away and hung up the phone. One of the families from the church was outside cutting the church's lawn, so I went and asked them to watch the kids and then took off.

76

I'll be honest. I was scared. It was my first death of a church member. I thought to myself, "What do I do when I get there? What can I possibly say to this woman who is so hysterical she can't give her name to a nurse?" I felt totally unprepared. I felt useless. I knew who I was and I knew what she needed and I didn't think I was very well equipped for this at all. I was struggling with that and even wondering if I hadn't made a terrible mistake going into ministry. I was sure of what she needed and deserved and I doubted that I could provide it. I remembered thinking it might help a little if I knew who it was. I replayed the conversation with the nurse over and over for at least a clue that would help me to figure that out: nothing. I really almost pulled the car over and turned it around, thinking, "I just can't do this."

Then it hit me. How did that nurse know to call me? I mean, here I was struggling to figure out who I was about to go visit, this unnamed, unknown woman so overcome with grief that she can't give her own name to the nurse. How did the nurse know to call me? Did she just randomly pick up the phone and start calling churches in a twenty-mile radius asking, "Are you Pastor John?" when someone answered? And did she just happen to guess the right church *and* the right name when I picked up the phone?

I knew that wasn't true. She knew exactly who to call. Which means that this woman, so torn up with grief she couldn't give her own name to the nurse, could give my name to the nurse. When this hit me, I did pull the car over. I sat on the side of the road for a brief minute and wrapped my head around that. I thought to myself that whatever you thought this whole ministry thing was about, whatever you thought it meant to these people to be their pastor, you were wrong. This is something very, very different. You better get your stuff together really quickly, because this is real. She needs you now not to be her friend, but her pastor.

The rest of the drive was a blur. I got to the hospital. I did not go right in. I sat in the car gripping the steering wheel for a quiet minute or two. I remember having one last conversation with the one who got me into this whole thing in the first place. I said out loud, "Ok God. I'm going in there. I have no idea what I'm doing. I thought about quitting on the way over here, but I'm not going to do that. I made you a promise, and I'm going to live out my promise to you. But here's the deal. You made me a promise that when I didn't have the words to say, you would provide them. You keep your promise and I'll keep mine." That having been said, I got out of the car, walked into the hospital, and found what was there waiting for me.

The nurse was not exaggerating. There Lori was. She was a mess. Her grief was palpable. I stayed with her. I went in with her to talk with and say goodbye to her beloved Fred. Over the next few days, I went and sat with her in her grief. I sat with Fred's family and listened to them all pour out their grief. I prepared myself for the funeral that came just a few days later. I went and visited with her after the funeral. Weeks went by. To this day, I have no idea what it was I said to her. I didn't know what mattered or how it mattered. What I do remember, in fact, what I can never forget, is that she eventually came back to church one Sunday morning. Instead of going into the sanctuary, she came and met me outside my office. She was crying. She held my face in her hands. She told me she would never have gotten through this without me, and then went and took her seat in the sanctuary.

Before I went in to lead worship, I sat in my office. I told myself two things. One, you learned you can do this. Hold your head up, and don't doubt that God walks with you. Two, stop playing. This pastor stuff is serious business. Whatever you thought these people needed you to be, you were wrong. Now you know. Get it together.

Mayview was my training ground. I was there eight years with some of the most beautiful people you could imagine. They loved me into ministry. It was they who taught me what it meant to be a pastor. It was there I learned about the power of pastoral authority. Timmy Wright's and Phillip Wagner's stories were cute, but something deeply serious hit me later after their mothers told me those cute stories: these precious little children think of me as God or Jesus. That's some heavy stuff. I had to tell myself, "Don't you dare take what you are to them lightly; and don't you dare do anything to abuse or betray this trust that they have given you." What happened to Lori, and what she needed from her church and her pastor, was my first great lesson in understanding what being a pastor means. Only after that did it dawn on me what kind of authority we are given, and what it can be used to do.

Authorization in Ministry

On the second side of this coin we call ministry is authorization. There is an assumption that every professional clergyperson who functions within the life of the Church does so with the permission and oversight of some other person or body. Often, this process of authorization will include years of Masters level education at considerable expense, a battery of psychological examinations, oral examinations by various interested and invested constituencies from local churches to seminaries to judicatory bodies to ecclesiastical councils, interviews by a local church or calling body prior to employment, and finally continued oversight after ordination by a body equipped and trained to test whether or not the authorized, professional clergyperson remains fit for ministry in and on behalf of the denomination in which she serves.

I belong to the United Church of Christ. I am a Conference Minister, which doesn't mean a whole lot to anyone outside the denomination. I often just tell people to think of me as a bishop. The analogy works, to a point. The more subtle truth is that our bishop is a team of twelve people, well balanced with lay and clergy. They are called our Committee on Church and Ministry. They serve for six years. Together, they examine every candidate for ministry, determining on behalf of the entire Church whether or not they are fit to serve in and on behalf of the denomination.

Theirs is an onerous, and yet noble, task. The work of oversight doesn't end with a pastor's ordination. Every clergy who holds standing in our conference is subject to the oversight of these twelve people. For almost eleven years, I have staffed these committees on behalf of the two conferences I have served. Before that, I spent the previous six years serving on, and eventually chairing, one of the Missouri Committees.

At my very first meeting as a young pastor on the committee in Missouri, we heard a complaint about inappropriate sexual activity on the part of one of our pastors working with youth at our church camp. Since that time almost eighteen years ago, there have been very few times when I have not been processing a complaint about one of our pastors. I have processed complaints about clergy sexually abusing their grandchildren, traumatizing their staff because they could not manage their anger, extorting funds from their members, counseling a husband while the clergy was sleeping with the man's wife, plagiarizing ordination papers, using stories shared by members in counseling sessions as sermon illustrations, and so, so much more.

Clergy have authority. There is never any question about that. Those with authority to serve in the name of the Church also have authorization. This means that the authority derives from somewhere other than the clergy person themselves. It means that once authority is granted, those who function with that authority will place themselves under the oversight of the authorizing body. It can be no other way. Even independent churches with pastors who function with a great deal of authority have some way of holding that pastor accountable.

In a nutshell, authority and authorization serve as fundamental elements of ministry. They are crucial to our current understanding of what it means to be a part of the professional clergy of the Church

Before I write any more about this dynamic and how it all may be shifting, I want to add something very crucial to this discussion. It can be easily misunderstood that the church as we know it has become top heavy. Postmodernity, as we have already discussed, does not value established authority and hierarchy. It may be more accurate to say, quite simply, they don't trust it. They believe the adage that power corrupts, and absolute power corrupts absolutely.

Because of that, many who critique the church accuse it of being too heavily invested in hierarchy. They see power structures, and the people who occupy positions of power and authority, as corrupt. They see the structures, rubrics, and processes that govern authorization and oversight as hurdles to be jumped over, hoops to jump through in order to satisfy some arbitrary whim that those in power establish. They also see those with oversight as some sort of watchful eye to live in fear of. They are constantly watching, waiting for you to slip up so that they can strip you of your authority.

When the Church acts with the authority it is given, when it uses the power it is afforded, there is often someone, or someones, on the other side of that use of power who resist or resent it. This can happen when a pastor vetoes the actions of a local church board or preaches a sermon that makes the members feel uncomfortable. This can happen when a seminary student who is examined by an ordination committee is deemed not fit for ministry. This can happen when a local church pastor is stripped of her standing following a substantial violation of her ordination vows or of the ethical code of ministerial conduct. This can happen when a bishop closes or sells a church.

Hierarchy, power, and authority have become pejorative terms in the postmodern mind.

This is what I want to make clear: no power is given, blessed, held, or maintained in the Church unless the body politic as a collective whole believes it exists for the common good. Even in denominations with an episcopal polity, with clearly centralized lines of power and authority located in one person, existing structures are maintained because, and when, the collective will of the people believes that this is the best way to protect and preserve the integrity of the Church.

I am a judicatory officer because I believe that the structure the Church has built is a means by which people of faith can be assured that those whom we authorize to serve them are safe, competent, trustworthy. I feel the need to say that unequivocally before I write about the postmodern's relationship to power and authority, and what that might mean for how they come to build something to sustain their faith.

All denominations that seek to serve the gospel have their orthodoxies, including those with a more congregational polity. All denominations have certain standards of belief and practice that must be preserved. I happen to serve in a denomination that prides itself on its openness, and we require all candidates for authorized ministry to meet some pretty high standards that can only come after years of preparation. Demonstrating a requisite understanding of who we are, from where we came, and what our core values are, is essential. These orthodoxies exist to preserve an aspect of the gospel seen as essential to a church's or a denomination's way of being.

All who serve in the name of Jesus must also serve people. The sick and dying will be visited. The anxious and the grieving will be counseled. The lonely and the distraught will be comforted. Those who are authorized will be given almost unlimited access to people at their most vulnerable moments. I don't know of any other profession that has this access. Doctors will learn things about the sick that no one else will get to know. Lawyers will be entrusted with information that no one else hears. Counselors and therapists will hear the storied details of our lives that we don't share with anyone else. It is entirely likely that a clergy-person will hear all of that.

I often remind our oversight committees that when they examine a candidate for ministry, they should keep in mind the first order of the Hippocratic oath: do no harm. I ask them to test whether or not the person they are examining for ordination is one who they believe will do no harm. Because they will be given unfettered access to people at their most vulnerable, the potential for real damage to real people is always present. Great care and caution must be taken for the sake of those beautiful, and often so fragile, people. Because of the authority invested in clergy by the Church, their words and actions are so very powerful.

In order to preserve its established orthodoxy and to protect the vulnerable, the Church recognizes and uses authority and authorization as the two sides of the same coin which is—recognized ministry. Any authority given to the leaders of the Church is authority granted by the body politic for the preservation of orthodoxy and for the protection of its people. I do not mean to suggest that power offered cannot, or has not, been abused. We both know it can and it has. I do mean to suggest that, in spite of that, and with the full awareness that abuses remain and will continue, the Church as a body authorizes the use of power for the sake of its mission. It has long been the case that when that power or authority is abused, steps are taken to remedy the abuse and to preserve the church's equilibrium and effectiveness as an agent for the common good.

Once authorized, the professional clergy of the Church are granted permission to function in a variety of ways and settings to which few others in the Church will ever be given access. They will baptize, confirm, marry and bury. They will be given access every week to a pulpit from which they will speak without restraint or interruption, saying whatever is on their heart or mind. They will enter hospital rooms and prison cells. They will be invited into homes and hear the confessions of husbands, wives, partners, sons, and daughters and be asked to hold what they hear in strict confidence. They will be allowed to weigh in on life changing decisions, and sometimes even be given the option of making those decisions for others. When people are dying, they will be invited to witness the passing of a loved one. In the presence of death, it is they who will witness and heal grief, hear the stories of the deceased, and tell the story of the dead at a service commending them to God.

In my second church, I had an elderly member named George who lived alone. He was a quiet and humble man who lived a very simple life. He showed up every Sunday in his denim overalls and his conductor's hat. He used to work for the railroads. One day, George ended up in the hospital. He would not leave it. He would drift into unconsciousness and not come out.

Out of the blue, shortly after he went to the hospital, I got a call from a friend of mine who was a trusted attorney in town. He asked if George and I had talked. I told him that we had. He said he had something very specific he needed to ask me about. He was being very careful. As a lawyer, he knew full well about privileged conversation and the need for us to respect confidences. He wanted to know if George had ever talked to me about dying. I said he had. He wanted to know if George and I had ever talked about how he would feel about lingering hooked up to a machine. I told him we had. He wanted to know if I would be willing to go into court and testify to the content of those conversations and have the court authorize removing George from life support. I told him I would do that.

I have often reflected on that moment in my ministry. I was the only one George had ever talked to about that. He hadn't even trusted his attorney with it. He never bothered to sign any documents, and had slipped into a coma and couldn't testify to his own wishes on his own behalf.

I have had conversations like that with many people over the years. This was the only time I ever had to go into a courtroom on a member's behalf and share their wishes in a court of law, under oath, to a judge.

Given what is at stake, sufficient preparation and continuous oversight has been seen by the Church as essential. Whatever hierarchy exists is owned collectively, and willingly, by the Church, despite its oft-heard protestations to the contrary. It serves the common good.

Postmoderns and the Role of Clergy

I am not so sure that the postmodern church is going to see this the same way. An inherent disdain towards and distrust of established authority could produce a very different way of being Church. I have to actually check myself at this point. My default language is to talk about "being Church." That is an indication of how embedded I am in my own paradigm. The truth is, postmoderns don't talk about building Church or being Church. That is not their vision. I have tried to teach myself to stop referring to the postmodern "church," and to think instead of communities of faith or "sustaining faith."

A paradigm shift designed to create a new way to meet the needs of the faithful is emerging. It will prioritize a very different set of core values, standard practices and norms, and functional behaviors from its leaders. It will also look to build a model for sustaining the faith that establishes and oversees whatever they identify as leadership by very different methods.

I'm going to take a bit of a detour here. I will try and establish the relevance of this detour shortly.

I have already written that I believe the Church exists for a purpose: mission. Leadership and discipleship, however we define them, are empowered for the sake of that mission. Mission doesn't emanate from, and exist for, the church. It is the Church that emanates from and exists for mission.

This is a greatly oversimplified ecclesiology that I am about to present, but let if suffice for now. My personal faith, my sense of call, and my understanding of the need for a church have become pretty simplified.

I believe that every human being is a child of God, endowed with inherent worth and dignity and deserving of respect.

I believe that God desires to relate to, or to be in covenant with, what God created and that Her need for right relationship results in a call to preserve the common good, or to borrow more biblical language, *shalom.*

I believe that the law that was given was not a restrictive means by which humanity was to be controlled, judged, put to shame, and then either condemned or redeemed based on their strict adherence to it. I believe, instead, that the law is a proscriptive response to the question, "How do human beings ever stand a chance of living together in harmony with one another?" Well, says the lawgiver, don't steal from one another. Don't covet each other's property or spouse. Don't kill each other. Honor your parents. Love your God. You get the idea.

I believe Jesus discovered an established power structure that used that law as a means of belittling, shaming, judging, and condemning. I believe he discovered some who used that power to engender fear. I believe he discovered some who, with that ability to engender fear and shame, took advantage of their power and made religion a very lucrative industry. I believe he rebelled against religion that was used as a means of some acquiring power, wealth, and prestige at the expense of others.

Jesus was a corrective to all of that. He reminded us that the law could be summed up in this very simple formula: love your God with all you heart, soul, mind, and strength. Love your neighbor as yourself. He ate with those whom the religious establishment of his time shamed. He gave them back some sense of honor, dignity, and worth. He recruited disciples who would learn to proclaim that same gospel, and sent them in mission to all the ends of the earth to share the good news of God's love and acceptance.

Here is what I believe: the Church's mission, its purpose, its reason for being is to be an agent of God's *shalom*. It exists so that people will come to understand and experience their fundamental value and worth. I believe that there are religious and non-religious people around the world engaged fully in that mission. Most of them would not in any way think of themselves as either related to the Church or disciples of the one called Jesus.

I believe that the Church is living out its authentic call when it lives out its call to proclaim the good news of God's redeeming and transformative love. I believe that we do that best when our interest is not in conversion, membership, or active participation in the institutions we build and fund to undertake that mission. I believe that true conversion takes place, and is sufficiently completed, when a person learns to love themselves in such a way that they can come to love others more fully. I believe that any response on the part of the Church to organize itself to effectively undertake that mission is a good thing.

I'm going to say one more thing about what I believe about the Church, and then return to my point about the role of clergy. Whether I believe this or simply observe it, I often experience the Church as a body whose mission can appear to be to preserve itself. I know you can argue that to preserve an institution built to undertake a mission is a way of preserving the mission, but I don't experience those two as the same thing at all. What's more important, postmoderns don't experience that as the same thing, either.

As a partial remedy to this, I have taken to asking church governing boards to begin every meeting by giving everyone a chance to respond to one simple question: since last we met, how has this church blessed you. It is a way of helping them to reclaim their missional grounding as a people of blessing. It is a way of reminding them that those who experience blessing can be a blessing to another. It is a way of inviting them to gather less to argue about how to handle to growing needs of an institutional body that needs money to run than to remind themselves of their call to be engaged in the kind of mission that transforms lives for the common good.

So, after all of that, back to my point about the role of clergy. In order to organize its collective effort to proclaim the gospel to all the world, the Church evolved into a highly organized, effectively maintained hierarchy that, at all levels, was built to ensure a faithful proclamation of the gospel. No one, myself included, can argue that this well built machine failed in its grand and noble task. I stand utterly in awe of what this organization has built through the centuries.

To be sure, there have been abuses. Those cannot be eliminated. All in all, what the Church undertook and accomplished is nothing short of breathtaking. In small chapels, in hospital bedrooms, in prison cells, in war-torn villages and bergs, in underground railroads, in the halls of parliament and congress, in homes built to care for children with no home or family, in hospice centers, in domestic abuse shelters, in homeless centers, in sanctuaries both plain and ostentatious, on college campuses, in foxholes, in foreign lands and to countless indigenous populations, the organization that is the Church was deployed to proclaim the love of God. Whether it could have done this with or without the institution it built is irrelevant. The fact is that it did build it in order to undertake this mission on such a grand scale, and it worked. For many, it still does. For many others, it doesn't.

Jesus changed a church whose upper management, enamored of its power and the prestige it afforded them, lost sight of its core missional calling.

Postmoderns could very well be undertaking something very similar. Some see the Church now as an institution that has grown too large for its own good. Some witness an abuse of power and authority and see it as endemic to the institution itself. Some experience the Church as more invested in its perpetuation than its mission. Some feel that investing in a model of church that gives clergy centralized authority compromises a core value of the postmodern: the experts are already in the room.

Not everyone feels this way about the Church. There are still many for whom the Church as it is currently constructed is exactly what they want and need. As long as that is the case, church 2.0 will and should exist, and do everything in its power to serve those people to the best of its ability.

The question is whether or not postmodernity will need to create a new model in order for them to sustain the mission for which the Church was called into being. Will a more mobile, a more adaptive, a more decentralized, a more flexible, a less structured, a less institutionalized, a less organized model need to be birthed, grow and flourish in an effort to recommit the Church to its call to transform lives for the common good?

There are those who are already fully committed to this. They don't want, they don't need, nor do they seek the permission of the institutional church. They aren't all that interested in fighting the institution, either. There is already a big assortment of somewhat isolated, but often very well connected, pockets all over the country who are living a very simple, very spiritual existence in a community of faith. They are motivated by both a personal desire to live a fulfilling and connected life along with a corporate need to engage in work and mission that makes a difference in someone else's life. Later in the book I will give some snapshots of a wide variety of these settings and what they are about.

For now, I want to say that they orient themselves towards authority very differently. Blame that on the postmodern's hermeneutic of suspicion towards authority. Blame that on the postmodern's need to have their experiences matter and their voices heard not just in the process of democratizing the church and society but in the actual educational process itself. To the extent that clergy are received as, perceived as, and/or commissioned as, authority figures, that is the extent to which the postmodern mind will be unable accept them as a good investment in their effort to change the world or to live a meaningful life.

I have already written about the fact that some of our churches are dying. I have written also about the likelihood that many of those churches are not going to be replaced with new ones. Some of the Church's missional needs are going to be undertaken by a whole new breed of Christians (the next three chapters will attempt to describe that new breed). I have written about church 2.0's experience of finding it more and more difficult to place our authorized clergy in full-time positions that guarantee them a sustainable life income. I have written about some conversations that leaders in church 2.0 are having about whether or not we can/should continue to require seminary students to incur large debts without a promise of income on the other side of their authorization. This is all very real.

I don't know what the figures are for other denomination but I am guessing they are comparable. In the United Church of Christ, there are six related seminaries. I was told about ten years ago by one of the seminary presidents that it would take a minimum of $100 million in endowments to sustain the future life of any one of those seminaries. Some were well on their way to that figure while the others were doing everything they could to get there.

I have been told by another seminary president that it costs UCC seminaries $48,000 per student per year. With tuition at $12,000 per year, that means our seminaries have to come up with $36,000 per student per year.

The last figure I was quoted told me that there are about 340 men and women currently engaged in active pursuit of their Masters-level education in the United Church of Christ. If we are going to engage, system wide, in meaningful dialogue about the role of and continuing need for professional clergy as the most effective means of living out our missional calling, we have to have another serious conversation about missional resources. I wrote about this in chapter 3—that is, about the need for the Church to collectively account for our shared missional resources. We also have to identify and own our shared missional needs. Are we wisely stewarding those assets for the sake of those needs?

Such an assessment must, I argue, include the wisdom of a single denomination perpetuating six institutions of higher education that will require $144,000,000 each to educate what is right now a total of 250 students. This discussion must include a deep, objective analysis of the degree to which the Church for the future is asking for a professional, master's level, authorized clergy whose oversight is maintained by another costly judicatory office.

I am not arguing for or against the need for an educated clergy. I do see, though, that church 3.0 is questioning that. I am not convinced that it is my role to tell them to stop. I have no doubt that whatever emerges to sustain faith through this paradigm shift; leadership of some kind will be called upon. Whatever shape that leadership takes, the faithful will ask certain things of them that require skill, craft, and creativity.

Church 2.0 is going to be around for a long time and will continue to meet the needs of some who still are fed by this way of being Church. It will continue to undertake the mission for which it was birthed. We will still need some of our institutions that were established to help this way of being Church sustain itself, including clergy, seminaries to educate them, and judicatory bodies to oversee them in that ministry.

I can't stress this enough, though. Whatever will be left of church 2.0 will be compromised greatly if we do not have honest conversations about which of our current missional assets are needed to sustain institutions and judicatory offices at levels more commensurate with actual membership totals.

Do we need educated clergy? Yes, but it has become obvious to me, and others, that we can no longer afford all of the ones that we currently authorize.

Do we need seminaries and institutions dedicated to the mission of fully preparing men and women to serve the Church well? Yes, but it has become obvious to me and others? that we can no longer afford all of the ones that currently exist. It is also obvious to me that the mission of some of those seminaries will have to change dramatically in order for them to be relevant—fully prepared to meet the educational needs of those called to serve in a postmodern world.

Do we need judicatory offices to authorize and maintain oversight of our clergy? Yes, but it has become obvious to me that we can no longer afford all of the ones that we currently fund.

Not only can we not afford them, what remains of church 2.0 doesn't need all of them to sustain its mission. The leaders of church 2.0 need to sit down as covenant partners who care more about the collective missional calling of the Church than the perpetuation of whatever is left of its institutional identity. If it doesn't, it will continue to fritter away the resources it has been asked to steward for the sake of its mission. Without the collective will to do this for the good of the whole right now, church 2.0 is abandoning its future to a Darwin's test of the survival of the fittest.

Some clergy will survive and keep their jobs and income. Others will not. Many who don't will enter their mid-life trained for a call and a career that can no longer provide them with an income. Some seminaries will survive, while others will be slowly forced to close.

Some judicatory offices will remain—enough to meet the needs of a way of being Church that I don't think is going to disappear but will prove to be the choice over time of fewer and fewer people.

We begin with a mission. We ask ourselves what it will take to sustain that mission. Over time, the Church has sought to rebuild itself when new movements emerge or paradigms shift. Some already experience the Church of the present age to be an impediment to fully living out their call to faith. Because of that, we may be living through just such a time when the mission requires something new to sustain itself.

In this new movement there are deep questions being asked about the role of authority and authorization, the two sides of the same coin that is professional clergy. For the sake of the mission, those questions need to be addressed by something more humane and mature than the simple living out of a Darwinian inevitability.

CHAPTER SIX

New Metrics

"...as the present now will later be past, the order is rapidly fading..."

- Bob Dylan

We should become more like McDonald's (by the end of this chapter, you will know what I mean by that).
How do you measure success? If you play baseball, you look at batting averages, RBIs, ERA, and a host of other statistics. If you own a business, you look at profit margin. If you are a TV producer, you look at Nielsen ratings. If you are a stockbroker, you look at how your investments compare to the S&P 500 ratings index.

What if you're the Church? By what set of metrics does the Church measure success?

Membership and Finances
Churches do a lot. Individual members, groups within churches, or partnerships of churches undertake some pretty amazing work. What they accomplish week in and week out is very impressive.

The Church takes responsibility for spiritual growth. It organizes meaningful worship experiences every week. It funds and provides logistical support for music programs as part of the worship experience. It plans and holds retreats. It provides professional support for pre-marital and marital counseling. It writes prayers and produces devotionals used by members in many ways.

The Church organizes mission. It collects money to support organizations that provide meaningful relief for the elderly, the orphaned, the abused, the dying, the mentally ill, the homeless, the imprisoned, the poor, the underfed. It helps build homes, centers, and staff to support the needs of many who are found wanting. They support global mission partnerships in almost every country in the world, building schools and hospitals, providing medical supplies, collecting funds to supply livestock, water, and food to every corner of the globe.

The Church changes lives. Individuals plagued by grief, loneliness, addictions, or anxiety find comfort and support in the relationships that are built in their churches. For many youth and children, experiences in church camps, mission trips, Sunday Schools, or retreats organized by their local church are cited by them as the only places where they are welcomed without judgment. Many people who have been ridiculed, derided, or shamed by others for years find acceptance and comfort in their church family. Parents who find coping with rebellious adolescents a challenge are grateful for the support and advice they receive from the church family. Countless multitudes have come to receive the simply news that they are loved and lovable as life-changing. This is the Church at its best.

We can relate stories of lives changed by inspiring worship, compassionate grief counseling, challenging mission trips, and a host of other important and meaningful ministries carried out by the Church.

The church as we know it, however, doesn't address the question of how to measure its success by any of these metrics. Church Council agendas, denominational year-end statistical forms, and annual reports given to church members at their annual meetings reveal what it is that churches pay attention to when addressing the question of success or validity. From among all things that churches do and pay attention to, they measure their success by two metrics: membership and money.

A church is considered successful if they have enough members to support the budget. A pastor is considered successful if she attracts new members to the church, presents a balanced budget to the members, and is able at the same time to attract funds into the church's endowment fund. Members are considered faithful if they do two things: attend worship and contribute money (in fact, most church bylaws state that in order to maintain your active membership and reserve the right to vote, a member has to attend worship at least once a year, and make at least one financial contribution to the church).

Church council agendas almost always begin with a report of finances. This not only helps the elected representatives evaluate the extent to which members are being faithful to their responsibilities, but it also gives them a sense of how well the pastor is performing and helps them form a context for decisions that will be made as the meeting progresses. Knowing the financial health of the church will determine later in the meeting what can be done, what should be done, and what can and now should not be done—because of financial health. This report on the financial health of the church becomes the first lens through which the health of the church is measured. It serves as an internal barometer that helps leaders assess whether or not the membership is satisfied. A drop in funds is often a signal that there is dissatisfaction, and that something must be addressed.

If the health of the church's finances serves as an internal barometer, then the question of membership gains or losses can often serve as the external barometer. If financial health is a tool for measuring how the current membership feels about the organization, then membership totals can help a church get a sense for how the community feels about the organization. Therefore, the second metric used to assess the health of a church is membership gains and losses. A church that is attracting new members can feel about itself that its mission is being accomplished, and that somehow people outside the current life of the church are being attracted to them. A healthy church will be able to report at year's end that they have attracted more members than they lost. A church that sustains over time yearly losses in membership will begin to question its own health. There is consistent disagreement amongst church leaders about whether or not churches that level off, that show neither growth nor decline over a period of a few years, are healthy or unhealthy churches.

These two metrics are very closely related to one another. It almost goes without saying that if you have more members, you have greater potential to collect more dollars. The healthiest churches by these metrics are those who can both bring in new members, present a balanced budget, and build endowments.

These two metrics have been almost universally accepted as the tools used to assess a church's success, health, and vitality. A church might experience inspirational worship every week, with the pastor preaching moving sermons that help shape people's lives and choirs performing stunning works of music within those services. A church might provide meals or shelter to the homeless. A church might organize events or plan programs each week that keep youth and children connected to people who love and mentor them. Pastors might meet every week with shut-ins, visit the sick and the dying, counsel the grief-stricken and stressed. At the end of the year, the most amenable measurements to adjudge a church's health and success will be how much money was collected relative to how much money was needed to sustain the budget, and how many members joined relative to how many died or transferred out.

I understand this. First of all, these measurements are quantifiable. The rationale behind it has its merits. I know that there are those among us who feel like this is too pedantic or mercenary for an organization dedicated to transforming lives and operating in the spiritual realm. While there is an argument to be made that somehow the church should be above just counting money and members, the fact is the church cannot be above paying attention to these factors.

I do not, by any means, want to suggest that churches only care about the amount of money that is collected and the number of members that are active. I am focusing here specifically on what churches do and say to answer questions about their health, success, and vitality. It is my consistent experience that churches focus on two very measurable, very quantifiable entities to help them get a sense of how successful, healthy, and vital they are.

Four Points

There are four points I want to make in this chapter. The first is that if we think that using these metrics to evaluate the success of the church's mission means that the church has become cold, calculating, and heartless then we are wrong. The second is that the church cannot function without an ability to fund its mission, nor can it succeed without men, women, youth, and children who are committed fully to that mission and who offer their time, talents, and resources willingly to support it. The third thing is that we have moved very quickly out of a time when churches had every right and reason to expect that if they were faithful, diligent, and motivated people would be attracted and into a time when already existing churches are having to compete with each other for what is left in the market for what they are selling. The fourth point is that what the emergent church is already trying to argue: that new metrics are needed, and that this may be an adaptation that church 2.0 is ill prepared to make.

Points One and Two

So, let's take at look at each of those. The Church is an amazing piece of work. It really does change lives, sometimes in the most incredible ways. I would not want anyone to think that the Church, as

94

it currently is constructed, is only motivated by counting money and members. Nothing could be further from the truth. The money and the membership are not ends in and of themselves. Whatever effort and energy the Church expends trying to grow their budget or attract new members is expended because of the impact the proclamation of the gospel has to change lives. The Church witnesses this and feels a strong calling to undertake its mission with passion, with zeal, with intelligence, and with integrity. It hears the testimony of those whose lives are changed, and it knows it has done something pleasing to God. It wants to do it again, and it is willing to offer time and money to make that happen.

A story, if you please. Its one of countless others I could tell, but it illustrates the point so beautifully. David West was about 18 years old when his family started worshipping at our church in Lebanon, MO. David fell in love with the church, and especially the youth programs there. He started attending every event held by our youth. David faced the challenge of some mental retardation and wasn't always understood or embraced. At First Congregational UCC in Lebanon, that was never an issue. The youth loved and adored him. He became an integral part of all that they did and he was never made to feel like he didn't belong.

When fall rolled around, David learned about the confirmation class that would be offered. He made a personal choice to be a part of that. His faith had come to mean a great deal to him. He attended classes every week. Everything he learned came as pure joy to him.

Toward the end of the confirmation year, we started talking to the confirmands about Presentation Sunday. In our church, confirmation was conducted on Pentecost Sunday. The week before that was Presentation Sunday, when each student would stand before the church, literally presenting themselves to the assembled congregation. They would read an essay they had composed that expressed the core elements of their faith as well as why they believed that on this journey into adulthood they were ready to claim it as their own.

David's family adored and loved him. He was so precious and dear to them. His father, Bill, was a man devoted to his wife and children. Bill was very proud of David and all that he was able to accomplish. He was everything you would want a good father to be. When David learned about Presentation Sunday, he asked to meet with me. He came to me as a proud and concerned father. He told me in essence that David, who so badly wanted to do what all of his peers were doing, could not write or read that essay with his classmates. He wanted to talk about what other options were available to him. He knew David had to stand up that Sunday and be given an opportunity to express his faith just like the others, but he didn't want his son to be embarrassed or belittled.

After talking our way through some possibilities, none of which seemed completely adequate or appropriate, we both promised to devote more time thinking about what would be most appropriate. A week or so later, Bill stopped by and asked me if I trusted him. I told him of course I did, and he just smiled. He told me he had it figured out, but wouldn't say any more than that.

Presentation Sunday would come. David would speak last. When his turn came to rise before the congregation and express his faith, Bill came with him. They both stood, side by side, in the pulpit. A respectful hush came over the congregation. There were no notes, no papers, no written words to guide David through this. At first I thought Bill was just there for moral support—to comfort David through his nerves. His role was much less passive than that.

Bill was the first to speak. "David, who is God?" David was clearly nervous. He was well aware of the crowd, of their focus on him, and of how important this moment was. He stammered out his response—not because he wasn't sure or didn't comprehend. He knew exactly what he was saying and what this meant. He was sure of his faith, and proud of it. But he was a little nervous. "G-G-God made me."

Bill was beaming. His smile was genuine. He spoke again. "And who is Jesus?"

"G-G-God's son."

"And what do you know about them?"

"They love me." No stammering this time.

That was it. When they finished and stepped aside, there wasn't a dry eye in the sanctuary. We had all just witnessed the most beautiful, most sacred, most genuine expression of the faith we could ever hope to hear. I never in my life preached a better sermon than that.

It was more than that, though. We also became deeply aware of how transformative genuine love and acceptance are. There stood this proud father, his beautiful son at his side, and could all see how much this meant to them. They had been loved. They had been fully embraced for who they were. They were accepted without question by a community of faith that not only let them be who they were called by God to be, but saw that it was good and right and lovely. Part of what we all felt that day was the satisfaction of knowing that the precious gift of love and acceptance they received was something we discovered we had the capacity to offer.

This is the Church. Say what you will about it, but even when it is counting its money and its members, it is certainly above only counting money and members. It makes a difference, a real and meaningful difference in the lives of many people.

Guess what? Money matters. Members matter. These profound differences we make in the lives of real people, they don't happen if there aren't other people present who both believe in the ministry of the Church to transform lives and who actively support that ministry with their time, talent, and money.

There is no doubt that churches make a difference. They matter. People truly rely on them for meaning, purpose, comfort, strength, nurturance, guidance, support, and encounters with the sacred. There is also no doubt that none of this happens without money and members.

Churches have budgets. Budgets require funding. Funding requires donors. Churches have to expect that, in order for their ministry to unfold, certain needs will arise and certain expectations must be met.

Depending on the size of the church, there will need to assemble a staff. Most begin with a pastor. The average price tag for a full-time, seminary trained, ordained clergy person today is somewhere around $85,000. Many churches will add some kind of support staff to put weekly bulletins and newsletters together, type up the official minutes of the church's meetings, build and maintain the website, log into the official church records all official ritual activities of the church (baptisms, weddings, transfers, burials, etc.), keep track of the membership list, help the pastor organize a visitation schedule, etc. Again, depending on size and need, churches may add an assortment of associate pastors, youth leaders, teachers, music directors, accompanists, etc.—all of whom have salary and benefits packages commensurate with their time and talent.

Churches also need property. They need office space for their staff. They need fellowship space in which to build meaningful community with each other. They need classroom space for educational and youth programs. They need a sanctuary that accommodates their worship needs and inspires those who gather.

Boilers give out, air conditioners fail, grass grows, carpeting gets worn, roofs leak, paint peals, water lines drip, electrical systems get old and outdated—and all of that costs money to maintain. Computers and programs, file cabinets, desks, altar cloths, telephones, copiers, light bulbs, office supplies all have to be purchased and maintained to keep a church office running efficiently.

Churches are rarely isolated bodies. They function within a network of support systems that work to mutually sustain one another. A percentage of their annual budget is siphoned off to help support those partners. Denominational structures rely on money collected from local churches to maintain their own staff, property, and programming. Mission agencies around the world from Habitat for Humanity, Church World Service, Heifer International, homeless and abuse shelters, children's homes, campus ministries, and literally thousands of others compete with each other for money collected by the members of local churches.

When councils, boards, clergy, elected lay leaders, judicatory officers, and denominational leaders talk about money and membership, they are doing honest and meaningful work for the church and its mission. It may not feel "sacred," but mission can't happen without either.

Mission never comes free to a church. It requires money in order to be sustained. The simple truth is, money is going to come almost exclusively from the membership of the church. There will be the assorted bake sales, rummage sales, auctions, and fund-raisers that help—but we all know that the budget is the responsibility of the members. Therefore, the focus on funding has to have a requisite focus on funders—in other words, members.

I want to be as clear as I can that when the church opts to measure its success by counting money and members, it is responding faithfully to the impulse to be engaged in the kind of meaningful mission and ministry that changes lives and helps sustain the common good.

Having said that, there are currently two challenges that the Church faces as it focuses attention on money and membership, which leads me into discussion about the third and the fourth points I want to make.

Point Three

I can't tell you how many consultations I have had through the years with clergy or lay leaders who envision some remarkable ministry that they are passionate about. They believe in their hearts that their new ministry will change lives. They are willing to sacrifice everything to bring their vision to life. They almost always have powerful stories about how the ministry has already made a real impact, a meaningful difference. The stories witness to the power of their vision. They just can't fund it.

This causes tremendous pain, grief, and frustration. Local church pastors and clergy who are engaged in meaningful ministry are finding it harder and harder to fund their mission. Whatever was built into the system before to sustain the ministry of our churches is proving insufficient today. Clergy who were trained to be pastoral counselors, preachers, and spiritual guides now have a whole new set of expectations placed on them: raise money, manage money, market, advertise, and attract new members.

Clergy are, by and large, ill-prepared for these tasks. Fund development, marketing, advertising, and growth strategies are specialized, skilled fields that take training and experience that clergy don't bring to the table. I know many who have taken continuing ed courses, attended seminars, read books, gotten executive level coaching to improve their skills in this area. The problem is, other not-for-profit businesses are run by professionals who went to business school and studied not-for-profit management. They have dedicated years of focused attention developing their skills. They have spent years in a profession that every day asks them to put those talents to good use.

For our clergy, this will never be their primary focus. They have worship to prepare, sick to visit, grievers to comfort, sermons to write, classes to teach, committee meetings to prepare for, elected leaders to prepare and train. This is what they do well. Theirs is a hard and noble task, and they undertake it tirelessly. The derive joy and satisfaction in the effort.

All of a sudden, it isn't enough. As budgets shrink and membership rolls decline, we now want our clergy to become CEOs, managers, marketers, and growth strategists. They are women and men who will do anything for the Church they love—and so they will add this to their portfolio. By and large, though, they aren't trained for or necessarily gifted at this. Even in their better weeks, these tasks won't be their highest priority—at least not as long as sermons need to be written, worship prepared, funerals to prepare for, sick and grieving to visit, youth programs to organize, Sunday Schools and adult educational classes to prepare for.

One of the things hindering the health and vitality of the Church today is that key leaders are well equipped to change lives in a time when churches also need them to fund mission. They are now called upon to develop skills to raise money and attract members. Pastors are very good practitioners of a noble calling, for which they have been well prepared. There was a time when that was enough. It doesn't appear to be enough any more.

Very few church leaders that I know accepted their call to ministry because of their business acumen. Something touched their heart and called them into ministry to change lives. This puts our professionally trained clergy in a very difficult position. They have become, in effect, CEOs of not-for-profit corporations in a very competitive environment. Churches now stand in a long line of organizations competing for the philanthropic dollars of their active members. It isn't a very fair competition.

Church clergy don't, as a general rule, have either a background or education in not-for-profit management. They are trained to preach, teach, counsel, witness, manage conflict, etc. The tricky art of fund development and membership recruitment isn't their forte. It is not where their passions lead them. Even when they devote continuing ed time and funds to learn more about it, they don't undertake it with the passion and zeal that other pastoral tasks engender in them. There are exceptions, of course—but they are just that, exceptions, outliers.

There may have been a time when churches didn't need their clergy to do any more than preach, counsel, visit, and teach. The social fabric of their members' lives were structured around their involvement in the church. Growth strategies amounted effectively to evangelism through procreation, so sophisticated membership drives weren't needed either. Those days are long gone. As we talked about in the first chapter, societal and cultural circumstances are affecting the growth capacity of the church.

Organizations competing for available funding resources outside the local church are often run well by professionally trained CEOs or executive directors. Churches are not. Baby Boomers stand to inherit trillions of dollars over the next 15 years. Many of them were idealists whose hearts were set on changing the world. In 2011, the first boomers reached retirement age. There is money to be had from these idealists, many of whom now look back on a life committed to far more mundane things than what their young idealism gave them reason to hope for. They still want to make a difference, and they believe their money can help them do that.

Every not-for-profit organization outside the church is fully aware of this phenomenon. Some of them have built and trained professional fund developers just for this purpose.

The Church is grossly underprepared to compete for these dollars. It is unwise of them to expect that in this competitive market, untrained and already exhausted, overworked clergy have the tools needed to compete successfully in this market. The Church has come out of a time of almost exclusive rights to charitable donations. At the very least, we have every right to expect that we would be fully funded by our members. We now have to wake up to the reality that our members are being cultivated by our competitors, and are giving vastly larger and larger amounts of money to them at the expense of the church contributions.

The Church is way behind the curve on this. We are in direct competition with some very talented, very well trained, and very committed fund developers representing an amazing array of not-for-profit, charitable companies. Not only are they better at marketing themselves; not only are they better at identifying potential impact donors; not only are they better at building towards and making the ask; they are often better at doing what we call mission.

Fundraising 101 teaches that there are three critical factors to inspiring potential donors. In order to create a successful opportunity for giving, an organization must effectively demonstrate three things to the donor's satisfaction: first, that it has a mission worthy of funding; second, that they have a leader that a donor knows, trusts, and respects; three, that they can manage the money in order to effect the mission.

In this new environment, churches find themselves competing with organizations who are very clear about their mission. They are led by well-trained managers who are very sophisticated at articulating that mission succinctly. These leaders have developed highly refined skills at marketing their mission to potential benefactors, cultivating with practiced technique relationships that over time build trust and respect. They know from the start the purpose of the relationship is to make what is called "the ask." The ask is not made until some very expensive computer data gives them a very good idea about the prospective donor's interests and giving potential. There is no sense of guilt or shame attached to this ask because they know full well that the mission that they are so passionate about can't exist without it.

When I say that these organizations are probably better at doing what we call mission, I don't mean to suggest that the Church doesn't do mission. It does. As I wrote earlier, what churches accomplish amazes me. I have made a habit over the last decade or so to ask key church leaders to tell me what their mission is. With very few exceptions, they can't do it. It isn't something they ever think about. They love their church. They know that something happens in that community of faithful believers that impacts their life. Maybe they even have memories of their church helping out at a homeless shelter, or delivering Christmas gifts to an indigent family. They certainly remember how when a loved one died, their pastor and their church family were there to see them through their grief.

Very few church leaders, though, can answer the first and most essential question every prospective donor is asking: what is your mission? There is a sad irony inherent in this: that churches built for mission can't name their mission. They can't answer in a quick sentence or two why it is God has called their church into being. They don't have what the industry calls their "elevator speech," (this is the response you give when someone on an elevator asks what your organization is built to do, and you only have until the door opens again to inspire them).

This isn't a critique I am offering here. Churches do what they do. They do it with passion, purpose, and dignity. They change lives. Their leaders and pastors aren't graduates of business schools. They didn't graduate from the Indiana University School of Philanthropy. Previous generations of church-goers lived in a culture where the expectations around giving were transmitted faithfully from one generation to the next. Members knew what that it was incumbent on them to fund their church's mission. They didn't want or need a pastor who had a business degree. They wanted a pastor who could shepherd them with love, care, and courage.

That church may not exist anymore. The current Church finds itself in competition for its members' resources at a time when a whole new industry of philanthropy and charity exists. Its leaders are in direct contact with the charitable givers who occupy church pews. They are in direct competition with the Church for resources held by Church members. They know their elevator speeches. They know without guessing what their mission is, and how it changes lives. They know how to make an ask and get results. They have developed these skills with great practice and precision. The Church is just not equipped to compete in this environment.

Point Four

I have been stating the case in defense of a church that focuses attention on money and members. It has to, in order to survive.

Guess what? In the end, it doesn't matter what I think.

I'm already fully invested in and fully committed to the Church. Whatever new growth is out there to be found is going to come from those who are not yet invested in and not yet committed to the Church.

For too many of them, there is a perception that the Church to which I belong has lost its missional core. It is seen as overly consumed with a fear about survival without a requisite and serious look at who, beyond its members, depends on its survival. They perceive that the delicate balance between legitimate fund-raising for meaningful mission has become a desperate attempt to find enough money just to stay open and alive.

The title of this chapter is "New Metrics." That title was chosen intentionally. It began with asking an important question. How do you measure success?

For many, it has become readily apparent that the Church as they see it measures its success by counting money and members. This statement, to the extent that it is true, is indicative to them of a church out of balance.

That the Church needs develop skills to raise funds and attract members is a given. The postmodern Church will face this challenge as well. The question about balance is an important one, though. When this becomes our measuring stick, our indicator of health and vitality, many will argue that we are out of balance.

At his address to Synod delegates in 2011, the Rev. Ben Guess talked about the centrality of mission. Ben is the Executive Minister of the United Church's Local Church Ministries. He is one of four Collegium members, elected denominational officials who lead the United Church of Christ.

In that address, he talked about McDonald's. He reminded us all that from the early days of our childhood, we remember driving by those golden arches and seeing one number followed by one word: "X-number served." The number has grown through the years, and will continue to for some time. That single word remains: served. No matter what they do, no matter how their menu changes over the years, no matter what new jingle or ad campaign their marketing team develops, the constant is that McDonald's knows it is in the business of *serving* their customers.

Ben wondered aloud for us what might happen if the Church reminded itself that we, too, are built for service. He got me, and many others, wondering about the possibility of every church, every Sunday, writing across its outdoor sign "x-number served."

Just imagine strangers driving by and reading one thing about your church: This week, 1,200 people were served by this church.'

It got me wondering what might happen if our Sunday bulletins did the same thing. Right there on the front page, in the upper right hand corner, one number and one word: 20,000 served.

It got me wondering what might happen if members came every Sunday to report to the deacons how many people they served that week. The deacons would collect those totals, and next week's bulletin, and the church website, would report simply "22,345 served this week." Members would leave the church asking what they were going to do that week to serve someone else. The list could include those who visit a shut-in, carrying someone's groceries to their car for them, speaking at the local Rotary about how your faith sustains you, mowing the lawn of an elderly neighbor. People will get more and more creative about what they count as service. The church itself will begin to shift their understanding of how to measure their success. That's the point!

It got me wondering what would happen if churches added five minutes to every service, and every week invited one person to talk about what they did in service to the gospel. They would not only share what they did, but they would also talk about how it affected them and how it affected the person or persons they served.

It got me wondering what might happen if every church then reported weekly to their judicatory office what their number is, so that this could be displayed on a meter kept on the front page of their website or reported on its Facebook page what all of the churches in that geography reported.

Then, under the number that reported last week's total service to the community, a second number would keep a running total in perpetuity, just like McDonalds does. How long before we hit 1 million? How long before 10 million? How long before 1 billion? These aren't just numbers—these are lives on both sides of the equation affected by being called into service: changed because of offering the gift, changed for having received the gift.

I think that churches, and their members, change lives weekly. I just don't think we pay that much attention to it. I think we have gotten stuck imagining that our health and vitality are measured not by lives served or changed, but by money donated and members active. I have already argued that those are important, but I don't think that they are the standards by which we measure a church's success. I have no doubt that our focus on those figures has left the emergent church feeling like we have, in some way, sold out.

This is an intriguing thought for me. Whether we ever try this, who knows? What I do know is that the Church today is seen, by many, as having lost its balance. There is little doubt in my mind that the emerging Church is being built in part as a reaction to their experience of seeing a church out of balance. It is in no small part due to that perception that one of the characteristics of the emergent church is a foundational reliance on mission. (There will be challenges for postmoderns to face as this model moves through its own stages of development. At some point, it too will have to struggle to sustain itself beyond being just a reaction to something else. There is authenticity in what these communities are doing to live out their faith. Authenticity does not guarantee sustainability, though. They, too, will have to face questions of funding their vision.)

I am intrigued by what Ben Guess is proposing. It is nothing short of a belief in the value of a new metric. It is a reasonable alternative response to the question about how the Church measures its success. It can be measured not in money collected, not in members gained, but in people served.

It certainly leaves open the possibility that churches that are small are not insignificant. It leaves open the possibility that even in times of numerical diminishment, churches can be proud of their success as a center for mission. It can help to remind churches that budgets don't get fed to perpetuate an institution, or to maintain building and property, but to fund mission. It can also go a long way to invigorate a church grown weary and stale from asking its key leaders to offer their time and focus their attention on finances, property, and membership. It gives permission to our leaders to do what inspired them to be a part of the Church in the first place.

The Church is the Church not when its bills are paid. The Church is the Church not when its pews are full. Those are nice things for a church to be able to say about itself, but they are not necessarily the metrics by which we measure our value, our worth, our success.

The Church is the Church when lives are changed. It is the Church when it inspires people to use their time, talent, and resources to serve the common good. It is the Church when it helps people love themselves, their God, and their neighbor. Developing new habits around measuring these successes could very be what the Church is called to think about.

CHAPTER SEVEN

A Growing Multiplicity

There's more than one answer to these questions
Pointing me in crooked line
The less I seek my source for some definitive
The closer I am to fine

- The Indigo Girls

I grew up Roman Catholic.

Until I met Dan Arnold, who lived behind me in the house I grew up in, I didn't realize that there were anything but Roman Catholics in the world. Turns out Dan was Baptist. I had no earthly idea what that was. The fences that separated our yards were about 30 feet apart. I will never forget how, one morning, we both sat behind those fences and asked each other questions about our respective faiths. I was deeply curious, intrigued. I was learning something that I sensed even then—I was probably eight years old at the time—was important: not everyone walks their journey in faith the same way.

I didn't know anything about religious tolerance at that age. All I knew is that Dan Arnold was my best friend. We played together almost every day. It was baseball in the apple orchard or the back alley during the summertime. It was basketball in his backyard or football in mine during the fall. It was hockey in the streets during the long winter months. We would ride bikes around the neighborhood, collect, compare, and trade baseball cards, and, sometimes, just talk. I loved the guy. The thought of him going to hell never crossed my mind.

My world was a pretty closed world. I lived in a quiet suburban neighborhood in northwest St. Louis County. I went to a Catholic grade school. I went to mass six days a week most weeks, and sometimes, when I was listed as an altar boy on the Saturday morning schedule, it was seven days a week. If it weren't for Dan Arnold living thirty feet away from our house, I could have gone my entire first decade of life without ever talking to someone who wasn't a Catholic. Well, that's not entirely true. I had many conversations with people who weren't Catholic; it is just that I never knew it. I assumed they were, and if they weren't, they never told me otherwise.

I knew some of the neighborhood children that went to public schools, but those same kids played on my soccer and baseball teams—teams sponsored by my Catholic Church. My home church sponsored and outfitted fifty-two soccer teams. Growing up in St. Louis meant playing Catholic sponsored youth soccer and baseball. I just assumed they were all Catholic.

Dan was a revelation to me. He introduced me to something outside of my sphere of understanding. He was a building block to what would develop into a postmodern mind. In his book *Postmodern Christianity*, John Riggs refers to postmodernism as "irreducibly plural." Dan Arnold was the first step in my world becoming irreducibly plural, after having been raised in one of the most irreducibly monocultural environments you could imagine in late twentieth-century America.

While I remember clearly that conversation with Dan, what I don't remember with precision or clarity is the genesis of the internal struggle that would evolve. I am now a Conference Minister in the United Church of Christ. Something happened. You don't get from there to here without some drama unfolding along the way (trust me, there was drama). Before any of it, before the thousand little things and the few not so little things that would conspire to open this pathway for me, there was Dan Arnold.

In the seemingly countless days of catholic indoctrination during my childhood, adolescence, and young adulthood I heard over and over again one of the teachings of the Catholic church: *ex ecclesia nula salus* (outside the church there is no salvation).

Clarity about these exact moments escapes me. I don't know when it was precisely that I heard this teaching for the first time. I don't remember when it was exactly that it dawned on me that if this was true, Dan Arnold could not be saved. I don't know exactly when that realization caused me to start thinking with a questioning mind about others things I was told to accept.

I probably don't have to do the translation for you, but I will. For me to accept this teaching of the church, *ex ecclesia nula salus*, I had to believe that my best friend, who had already demonstrated to me that his faith in Jesus was as deep and profound as mine, was going to hell. Worse than that, his going to hell was a part of a code authorized and approved by the God I worshipped. That rocked my world. Early seeds of rebellion against the religion of my childhood were planted somewhere in that dirt.

This was not an epiphany that woke me up. It just didn't unfold that way at all. It was a long, slow process that evolved over years. My acceptance of Catholicism wasn't something I thought at all about. It just was. I don't think to breath. I don't think about my right foot going two and a half feet in front of my left when I take my next step. I don't think about why I put cloths on every morning. Some things just are—and because they are you don't question or even take notice of doing them or not doing them.

Catholicism was like that for me. It just was. It would take a long, long time for me to realize that there was a market place of ideas competing with one another in my own mind, and that I had choices. Even when they started to emerge, I fought them hard for a long time. I think I even saw them as tests, temptations to stray which a good boy must resist.

Over time, I just could not reconcile what I felt about my childhood pal with what I was being taught. I would spend eight years in the Catholic seminary. Priesthood was not just my childhood dream; it was my calling. I didn't doubt that at all.

Questions just kept coming, though. These questions had me seeking desperately for answers that would help me reconcile my emotions with my faith. The strongest emotion was trying to reconcile with a God who had taken an interest in condemning my best friend to hell. I believed that the church had to know something that I was missing that would help me make sense of these things, and so I kept pushing for answers. I suspected it was I who had things mixed up, and that someone would say something that help me understand it. As long as I believed that, I hung in there.

It was a painful, a very painful, day when I realized that what I believed and what the church was asking me to believe could not be reconciled. It meant giving up my call to be a priest. I knew that was coming years before I would let myself believe it. I knew I could never, with any kind of integrity, pledge a vow of obedience to my bishop that would require me to require others to believe things that in my own heart had not yet come to believe. I was, without the vocabulary to articulate it, becoming irreducibly plural. I had to find a spiritual pathway that would accommodate this plurality, and it wasn't going to be in the faith of my childhood. I have Dan Arnold to thank for that.

I also have Dan Arnold to thank for my wife—in a very, very roundabout way. Even before I fell in love with her, I knew she was

Lutheran. I had already wrestled with my expanding pluralism. The thought of spending the rest of my life with a Lutheran brought no internal conflict to my heart whatsoever. Our relationship blossomed without the sometimes debilitating argument about whose faith would be practiced in the relationship.

Just as wrestling with what the church had to say about Dan would eventually lead me to leave seminary, falling in love with Mimi, the Lutheran, led me to walk away from my Catholic roots altogether and choose another spiritual pathway. There was never any anti-Catholocism in this for me. It was just that I had come to accept that being a disciple of the one called Jesus was no less authentic for me as a Lutheran.

I was often asked after that why I left the church. The question came from all of my old Catholic friends. My response took them by surprise: I didn't. I was as much a part of the church as a Protestant Lutheran as I ever had been while a Catholic.

Post-Christian

My story is a familiar one. Life experiences for postmoderns explode assumptions long held by those who preceded us. Most prominent among them is the assumption that whatever group, tribe, culture, or faith to which you belong is the norm against which all others are judged. Our world has grown so much smaller than it once was. It is certainly possible to live as if your worldview predominates, but it is harder and harder to do that and not collide with people close to you who have a very different perspective. The circle of meaningful relationships for postmoderns has become so richly diverse that parochialism, nativism, chauvinism, racism, and spiritual exclusivism are getting harder and harder to defend without challenge or ridicule. It is certainly harder to defend those impulses without jeopardizing meaningful relationships.

Postmoderns are highly suspect of organizations that want to justify their existence by condemning others. Postmoderns, by and large, don't buy into the concept of "joining" or becoming a "member" of any organization, in part for this very reason. Postmoderns are, to some extent, samplers. They want experiences that take them out of comfort zones, that expand world-views, and that enrich lives.

Being enticed down a spiritual pathway that requires them to brand themselves as Lutheran or Episcopalian or Methodist or even

Christian not only far less appeal to postmoderns, it is often the very reason they walk away from the church.

Postmodern Christianity is already in the process of becoming a Post-denominational church. While I don't think denominations are going to go extinct any time soon, I do think we are going to see mergers, partnerships, and downsizing as denominations realize over time that they are attracting fewer and fewer customers to the marketplace they currently occupy.

Calling postmodern Christians "post-denominational" is a way of saying that their expression of Christianity will resist any attempt to define it in a way that results in either a separation from others seeking spiritual sustenance, or even worse requires a presumption of superiority over them. It's not that postmoderns fear differentiation. It is more that they don't want to invest in anything that inhibits meaningful relationships with others who have a different set of beliefs or a different worldview. Differentiation is important. This is who I am. Tell me who you are. Let's explore how a relationship might affect our assumptions about that.

Calling postmodern Christians post-denominational is also a way of distinguishing it from the current model of the Church. Church 2.0 has learned that it is important to claim a pathway that is uniquely Methodist, or uniquely Lutheran, or uniquely Presbyterian. Whether by design or by accident, and I am sure there is plenty of both hidden in our histories somewhere, church 2.0 is set up in such a way that it isn't enough that you brand yourself a Christian. "What kind of Christian are you?" is an important question for the Church as it is currently structured.

Calling postmodern Christians post-denominational is also insufficient. It indicates that they are not going to invest in a model of the Church that brands one expression of Christianity as different from or better than another. It's important to know that about the postmodern Christian. It's also important to know that if that's all you know about postmodern Christianity, it isn't enough. Postmodern Christianity is also post-Christian.

We have to be careful here. Post-Christian isn't anti-Christian. It is, however, a way of fully expressing a fundamental commitment to the way of Jesus without any need or desire to see that as the only way or the better way. It is simply a way. There is a ready acceptance amongst post-modern seekers to see other pathways as legitimate. There is no need to argue that because a pathway is authentic for me, your choice is reduced to that as your only legitimate option. Most postmoderns go even further than that. By accepting Christianity as a pathway to pursue their faith authentically, they are not only saying that other options are legitimate for other people, they are saying other pathways are legitimate for them. Postmodern Christians are willing to explore what they can learn from the Jewish faith, the Hindu faith, the Muslim faith, etc.

This means that the postmodern Church is going have a hard time with a Christianity that expresses itself in such a way that the Hindus, the Muslims, the Jews, the agnostics, or the atheists are made to feel either unwelcome or inferior.

For this very reason, church 2.0 is going to feel like an alien church to most postmoderns. I preached at one of my Southwest Conference churches not long ago. Remember, I serve the United Church *of Christ*. I had chosen a gospel passage, and it won't surprise you to hear that Jesus was featured prominently in the story. He showed up a couple of times in my sermon.

When the service ended, a woman from the choir came over to me and told me how disorienting it was for her to hear so much emphasis on Jesus. She was very concerned that the atheists who worshipped with them would be offended.

I want to spend a little time unpacking that moment, because it is one of the most telling examples of one way of being Church colliding with another way of being Church.

Jesus Triumphant

The church that I grew up in, that I was educated in, and that I have been professionally trained to lead in is a Christian church that sees Jesus triumphant as all of the following: the way, the truth, and the life; the means of attaining salvation; the Son of God, fully human and yet supremely divine; a miracle worker; a prophet (but be careful not to say that in a way that would lead anyone to assume that he was just a prophet, or that his way of being prophet wasn't far superior to all others who took on that role before and after him); one who hears and answers prayer; present in the breaking of the bread, or where two or three are gathered; friend— and really, so much more.

There is inherent in all of this an understanding that while other faiths, other religions, and other spiritual pathways might have the potential to lead people to enlightenment, it would be a sacrilege to

112

speak, act, or teach in ways that would suggest that they are anything but inferior to the one true faith. Jesus is God's best self-expression. At its extreme, Christianity teaches that without a foundational belief in Jesus as the Son of God, there is nothing but eternal damnation awaiting. Even when Christianity is more progressive or tolerant, there is still an irreducible belief that those who don't know Jesus are missing something. They can still be good people and live meaningful lives, but if they knew the real Jesus they would see the light and come to accept him as the better way.

For the longest time, I was conditioned to feel sorry for those who had not yet come to believe in Jesus. As a Catholic, of course, that pity emanated from a knowledge that, without a basic belief in Jesus, eternal condemnation awaited.

With the pity came a naive sense that those who didn't believe just hadn't been given enough information about or experiences with the risen Christ. No one who had been granted the privilege of a personal encounter with Jesus would deny him—and if they did, well, they deserved that hell they were getting. This notion grew to the point that any person who died without having received Jesus was somehow my fault. I had failed them. With greater effort, zeal, or powers of persuasion, I could have made the difference for them. Had I done a better job as a true Christian, no one to whom I offered the invitation to accept him could deny him.

There are varying degrees to which Christianity still functions this way, even if I don't. It has been the predominant worldview for most churches for a very long time. No study of the history of the Church would be complete without an acknowledgement that this theology, combined with the power of the sword and state since the time of Constantine, has wreaked havoc on the globe. Colonialism, white power and supremacy, Manifest Destiny, the Crusades, Global Expansionism, and the Holocaust are all examples of how oppressive and unjust the church can be when it allies itself with empire.

Here are excerpts from the *Requerimiento*, a document written by the Spanish monarchy in 1513, and based on a Papal Bull written by Pope Alexander VI in 1493. The Papal Bull declared that the whole world was sovereign to God's ruler on earth, namely the pope. The *Requerimiento* was a declaration of war issued against any sovereign power that dared to think that whatever land it controlled belonged to them. It was read in Spanish by the 'explorers' funded by the King and Queen of Spain. It argued that since all lands belong to the pope, and they are there as his representatives, they are authorized to enforce sovereignty or to conquer the inhabitants of the land. These are excerpts:

> On the part of the King, Don Fernando, subduer of the barbarous nations, we their servants notify and make known to you, as best we can, that the Lord our God, Living and Eternal, created the Heaven and the Earth, and one man and one woman, of whom you and we, all the men of the world at the time, were and are descendants, and all those who came after and before us.

> Of all these nations God our Lord gave charge to one man, called St. Peter, that he should be Lord and Superior of all the men in the world, that all should obey him, and that he should be the head of the whole Human Race.

> One of these Pontiffs, who succeeded that St. Peter as Lord of the world, in the dignity and seat which I have before mentioned, made donation of these isles and Tierra-firme to the aforesaid King and Queen and to their successors, our lords.

> Wherefore, as best we can, we ask and require you that you consider what we have said to you, and that you take the time that shall be necessary to understand and deliberate upon it, and that you acknowledge the Church as the Ruler and Superior of the whole world.

> If you do so, you will do well, and that which you are obliged to do to their Highnesses, and we in their name shall receive you in all love and charity, and shall leave you, your wives, and your children, and your lands, free without servitude.

> But, if you do not do this, and maliciously make delay in it, I certify to you that, with the help of God, we shall powerfully enter into your country, and shall make war against you in all ways and manners that we can, and shall subject you to the yoke and obedience of the Church and of their Highnesses; we shall take you and your wives and your children, and

shall make slaves of them, and as such shall sell and dispose of them as their Highnesses may command.

In case you missed that, Spanish armies would land, meet the natives, read this document in a language they did not understand, force them to relinquish the land and convert to the one true church. If not, they would face forced servitude, exile, torture, banishment, and death—all in the name of Jesus.

This was an extreme. Not all who espouse a fundamental belief in Jesus as the way to eternal salvation take their powers of persuasion quite this far. It should be noted, however, that the amount of human degradation and suffering caused by those who do or did take it to this extreme cannot be calculated. It should also be noted that the same impulses that forced me to wrestle with the thought of Dan Arnold going to hell are the same impulses that birthed the Crusades and the Holocaust. From the Inquisition to the Crusades to Colonialism to the Pogroms to the Holocaust, the Christian Church's zeal to conquer and convert has left a trail of bloodshed, violence, and injustice throughout its history.

The Tao of Postmodernity

Postmodernity wants none of that. Postmoderns have lost their thirst for blood. To say that there is extant an embarrassment about what hath been wrought in the blessed name of Jesus would be to grossly understate the case. There is a shame that compels a new breed of Christian to live an irreducibly plural life. There is a strong desire to produce in the Church new impulses. Those impulses, borne of that irreducible pluralism, are to place Christianity alongside all the great religions of the world as an equal at its best and as admittedly far inferior at its worst.

Spirituality, faith, and religion exist to elicit a sense of awe and wonder toward the ineffable, the mysterious, the inexpressible, the sacred, the divine. They exist to engender a genuine sense of self worth and dignity. They exist to create a desire to offer one's life or talents in service to the common good. They exist to remind us that at our best, we love one another and treat our brother and sister they way we wish to be treated by them.

Almost every culture has discovered the sacred or the divine and experienced that presence as life giving and life affirming. Those experiences engender ritual, discipline, narrative, and faith. The practice of that faith, the rehearsal of that narrative, the undertaking of that discipline, and the acting out of that ritual serve to help human community evolve in peaceful, loving, and generative ways. They help us process grief and shame, and meet the new day with some sense of hope or with some tools to cope.

In his insightful work, *The Evolution of God*, Robert Wright observes that more and more people are getting intertwined in non-zero-sum relationships. That is a brilliant observation. As we continue to rely more heavily on each other, our cultural evolution requires of us a greater sense of cooperation, tolerance, understanding, and acceptance. Robert Wright believes that "the prospect of successfully playing a non-zero-sum game breeds decency." To borrow John Rigg's language, it breeds "irreducible pluralism." This is the world of the postmodern, and whatever expression of faith emerges in their new paradigm will bear witness to that.

Post-Christian Christians will be a strange, almost unrecognizable breed when viewed from the perspective Churches 1.0 and 2.0. Gone will be the impulse to preach, convert, and baptize non-believers for the salvation of their mortal soul. Gone will be the Christology that needs Jesus to be sovereign or savior. Gone will be the inclination to reduce all authentic spiritual truth to what the Bible can tolerate.

In its place will be a church filled with disciples of Jesus who walk in his way, and who do their best to be faithful practitioners of all that they understand him to have been. They will be more comfortable with a seated Buddha on their desk or mantle than with a cross (have one on my desk). They will attend services at temple, synagogue, mosque, sweat lodge, and church. They will baptize those who find that meaningful, but will never think differently about a fellow disciple of Jesus who doesn't see anything meaningful in that ritual. They will read from the Qur'an, the Bhagavad Gita, Confucius, the Vedas, and many other spiritual texts. They will consult spiritual directors, life coaches, mentors, rabbis, imams, priests, shamans, and others who demonstrate a capacity to put them in touch with the sacred.

Remember the woman that met me after I preached my sermon in her church, and who felt I may have offended the atheists that join them on Sunday morning? This is she. She is already living out that sense of irreducible pluralism. She is a postmodern. So is her church. In the same worship space that her community uses on Sunday morning a Jewish congregation worships on Saturday morning, and then an independent Catholic church pastored by a female priest worships on Sunday evening. Meanwhile, a drum circle of Native Americans gathers on the parking lot during every new moon for their own spiritual sustenance, and their spiritual guide uses the church for her office space.

For many, this is too much. Their brand of Christianity cannot go that far. For others, their worldview has shifted and the vessel built to contain modern Christianity no longer holds them. Their choices are to abandon Christianity as it currently exists or to reinvent it. Many have opted for the former, but so many others are attempting the latter. I stand among those who wish the latter the best. I hope like hell that, inspired by the sacred, the divine, the holy, they complete the task. Because if they don't, for more and more people with each passing year, there really only will be one option.

In each of the next four chapters, I am going to describe a postmodern community. They are all very different. They have unique characteristics that differentiate them from one another. This is far from a comprehensive look at the postmodern faith community. I am not sure that such a look can be fully exposed. It is, however, a glimpse—and an important one.

When I did my research for this project, I wasn't just exploring the new. I wasn't only asking questions about what was different and why. I was exploring something with far more meaning for me, personally.

I have come to understand that my role as a middle judicatory officer for the institutional church is not to preserve the institution or any of its component parts. My role is to preserve the unique proclamation of the gospel that made this expression of the Church necessary in the first place.

That's the deeper question I was asking. It wasn't "Who are you?," although I did get some insight into that. It wasn't "What motivates you?," although learning about those motivations turned out to be important. It wasn't "How do you undertake your mission?," although there is much to be learned in exploring that very question.

No. It was something much more basic than all of that. The question I went looking to resolve was this: can we trust the gospel to these outsiders?

That's offensive language—I know that. I own that. Nonetheless, that is the big question underlying all the grief, the anxiety, the fear of the institutional church today. We are dying, goes the oft-heard refrain. Behind that lies a deeper fear: will the gospel die with us?

These stories are told both as a response to the more utilitarian questions about who and how and why, but far more importantly as a response to the far deeper question about succession. I can only hope that as I report what I experienced, the reader will come to trust as I did that the gospel as we know it is in good hands. It is my hope that your own explorations of these postmodern communities of faith are no threat to the current expression of the Church and, in fact, are going to preserve the good news and make it relevant in people's lives in ways my church can't.

This is very gratifying to me. In the end, this was an exploration of hope after a time when decades of diminishing capacities had eroded hope. My time with and among these innovators came as a blessing to me. What happened was nothing short of my own personal transformation: from despair to hope; from confusion about a way to clarity of purpose and intent; from sorrow and deep grief to joy and abiding promise.

CHAPTER EIGHT

Reimagine

"You may say that I'm a dreamer, but I'm not the only one."
- John Lennon

Just south of Cesar Chavez Street in San Francisco, at the corner of Precita Ave and Alabama, across the street from the lovely Precita Park, sits the Precita Park Café. It's hip. It's trendy. It's menu has items like organic oatmeal, the divine veggie (hummus, mmm), and spring onion confit. The walls are covered with the works of local artists. Of course, that's where I met with my first innovator.

Dani Scoville is an absolute delight. Her smile is warm. Her enthusiasm is infectious. Her passion for the faith is unapologetic. She's a twenty-something post-modern woman with clear passions for the gospel and little attachment to the accouterments of the establishment Christianity.

She is a disciple of Mark Scandrette, founder of ReImagine, a postmodern community of faith serving the greater San Francisco area. While I was disappointed that Mark was not able to join us, I was grateful for the time I got to spend with his able and accomplished cohort. Her passion and enthusiasm for the work of ReImagine as well as her incredibly resourceful awareness of who they are and why made the time with her in that café pass rather quickly.

We can't, and I won't, call ReImagine a church. That part of the vocabulary doesn't work easily when we begin to talk about postmodern communities of faith. It has taken be a while to disabuse myself of the notion that we are talking about new churches here. We aren't.

ReImagine *is* a faith-based, non-profit organization built to explore how the details of Jesus's life are made manifest in our daily living. This is what they do. They find ways to explore Jesus, to learn what they can about who he was, what he did, and why.

These explorations are not idle ruminations. It is expected that insights will produce something meaningful for the whole person. These faithful explorations will inform how we eat, how we enter into relationships as a whole person, how we engage our sexual selves in relationship, how we relate to money, etc.

119

These explorations are engaged in workshops, in story telling, in mentoring, on retreats (some of those silent retreats, harkening back to some of the earliest threads of Christianity), weekly prayer gatherings, and community activities that are thoughtfully chosen so as to make a real difference. They recognize that they are a part of a community and that choices they make about how they live their lives will always have an impact. They want to know that their impact serves the common good.

There are about 15 people who have connected through the various offerings of ReImagine who gather weekly in what they refer to as a "tribe." (An interesting side note here is that a whole new vocabulary is developing. Each emergent community finds language that works for them. There is no expectation that one group will adopt the vocabulary of another. What we would see as a "congregation" might be a "tribe," a "cohort," a "gathering," etc.) The tribe meets in the home of one of the participants.

Participants take yearly vows. Having attended one of the workshops, or retreats, or having been mentored—all are asked to consider what promises they will make to help them walk in their community as Jesus walked in his time and place.

Each year, people are invited to sample from a variety of theme-related experiences. Every year, a familiar cycle of themes will be repeated but with different material – promising new experiences and new insights each time around.

Storytelling is very important to the life of ReImagine. Every Storytelling experience is different. Five people are chosen to prepare a story on whatever the subject matter might be. The story relates an experience from their own life. As the evening unfolds, everyone is given an opportunity to respond.

I pause here for a moment. I want to note the contrast between this truly postmodern community and what those who have grown up in the institutional model of the Church experience relative to the telling of our stories. This is an important place to note the difference between church 2.0 and church 3.0.

I don't want to suggest the church 2.0 does not give any time for people to tell their stories, but I do note it is not the norm. When we gather, we empower the ordained, authorized, and educated pastor to tell the stories of the faith. She has the training and expertise. The rest of us sit as passive recipients of their wisdom. We are not asked to respond. Our liturgies do not create space for response—other than whatever personal and private commitments we make to leave the service and live as Jesus would have us live based on what we heard the expert tell us.

I make this observation without judgment or commentary, only noting for the reader what I have discovered to be an important distinction. In sharp contrast to that, ReImagine gathers and asks give different people each time to tell THEIR story, informed as they see it by the life of Jesus. Those stories are followed by an invitation to the gathered to respond. The response might be an affirmation, a commitment, or another story.

Each month, ReImagine catalogues the "longings of our community." These longings will shape the prayer life of the participants. Practitioners of church 2.0 will recognize elements of their own prayer practices here. The naming of joys and concerns in worship gives voice to a prayer offered by the pastor in worship. I note that the postmodern community does not ask the pastor to take on their voice and speak for them. They catalogue the longings of their community. Those longings are named and owned by them as members of that community. They form the basis of their prayer life for the coming month.

At this point in my conversation with Dani, I heard a familiar refrain. Its one that church 2.0 has been living with for some time now. She told me "Sustainability is a question." Unlike most churches 2.0, almost every postmodern community of faith I visited has a very different understanding about how to fund their ministry.

At ReImagine, there were no offerings taken. Some of their programs are fee for service based and help cover expenses. Others are not. They are donor based, and income comes from any who find value in what they do and are willing to contribute. Those who have had meaningful experiences with them contribute at various levels. The staff of this postmodern community comprises the founder, Mark Scandrette and, at times, his wife Lisa, and Dani.

They are a "church of sojourners." At times, this is helpful for them. They don't own space. What they need they rent, cheap as they can get it—and often in exchange for some of the training they offer.

Retreats are held twice a year at a nearby camp. The retreats offer some silence, some guided meditations, time for deep contemplation. They will debrief with retreat participants. Packets are prepared ahead of time for them. Usually 20-25 people attend. Many of them will return to repeat the experience.

Mark is himself a seminary graduate. Dani is not. She has taken some classes and uses Mark as a mentor. I found her to be a very adept and articulate theologian. Her grasp of relevant scripture passages was evident to me throughout the conversation. In her own words, she believes she is technically "in ministry." She officiates at weddings, and no one cares that she is not ordained and did not go to seminary.

Here again we find a line of demarcation. It is here that I think church 2.0 will have its greatest struggle with what is emerging. Clear, historic, and well-reasoned commitments to the education, authorization, and oversight of all clergy ARE going to give way to what postmodern communities are already practicing. The simplicity and ease with which an individual recognizes and accepts the authenticity of another person's spiritual gifts will transform the nature and role of ministry in the postmodern church. This particular dynamic was observed in every setting I encountered – even in ones where the identified leaders *were* seminary trained, ordained, and authorized. In the postmodern church, the participants themselves don't ask for or require that.

If there is anything at all that smacks of evangelism, it is simply that others see the way that they live and desire to live that way themselves. Conversions, baptisms, membership drives are not a part of the culture or vocabulary. Their primary concern is that people learn to live as Jesus taught us in the hopes that communities discover a new capacity for peaceful living. Baptisms, confirmation rituals, membership drives are an impediment to the focus on simply living faithfully.

Within the house church element of their experience, the 'tribal gatherings,' leadership is shared. Home venues are rotated. All give and lead communion. The table fellowship is shared. It is sacred. It is a regular part of their worship experience.

Scripture is used. It informs the choices they make.

ReImagine takes on many shapes and sizes. There are many groups of six to eight that form and gather in homes. Two of their groups have grown to as many as fifteen. They change constantly. I am amazed, really, at the ease with which these communities have grown comfortable with their fluidity. They are, by their own admission, not very stable in any sense. Every month they will have a "family meeting" on a Sunday. At that meeting, they will discuss and figure out who has responsibility for what.

For the in-house worship, the groups of six to eight that will form gather for dinner. They work hard to finish at an appointed time because many have children and other responsibilities, and they want to honor that. There is often some agenda to the gathering, determined largely at the family meetings two months in advance. Scripture will be read, followed by a time of meditation. The meditations will have participants focusing on the vows they have made. The vows are offered in seven categories: prayer, community, service, creativity, simplicity, love, and obedience to God. There is a clear emphasis on discipline, and of submitting one's way of living to the way Jesus chose to live. The gatherings of tribe are held in living rooms. They use gluten free bread and wine for communion. Whoever serves tells others how the gifts will be shared and distributed, who will take and bless it, and what will be done to bless it.

Most of the people who have remained attached to ReImagine were in church at one time, and are "recovering" from the experience. That is a very common refrain among postmodern worshipers. Because of that, their experiences with sacrament are intentionally informal.

The ritual of this community is found in their weekly prayer routines. Those who can, join Marc in his home for prayer on Tuesday mornings. They read from the lectionary, followed by 20 minutes of stillness, silence, contemplation, and prayer. Prayer requests are spoken out loud, followed by the phrase "Lord, hear our prayer." They end with the Lord's Prayer.

Workshops are all built around the seven themes and the seven vows that accompany them. Each theme is dealt with around a workshop that is lead for six weeks on Tuesday evenings. They are held in homes, and when they can get it and need it in a church setting. In the fall, the theme is always simplicity; in the New Year, creativity; during Lent, obedience and discipline; in the late spring, community.

There is a mix in the workshops of people from the various tribes and others from their social network, some who have responded to their Facebook posting. There are always new faces and familiar faces when they gather for the workshops. They focus on what they hear the Bible saying to them, and how then they are called to live that out in their daily lives. They try hard to identify from where their resistance to live more faithfully comes.

In everything they do, they refrain with intentionality from identifying or being limited by a certain theological framework. The focus is on a radical openness to where God is found on the journey. If there is a reference point that grounds them, it is this: we are the beloved. They never use shame or guilt as a motivator. To quote Dani, "We are not shit with snow on it."

They all have their struggles, and try hard to remain faithful to what God has called them to be. They want to live out of the joy of recognizing that God loves them.

They will not engage in behaviors that ostracize. They want all to experience the healing of God. They work hard to create a safe space within which people's stories can emerge.

Shortly before I met with Dani, ReImagine did a storytelling evening on Sexuality. Those who were invited to tell their stories were given permission to simply begin by saying "Here is my story." All perspectives were included. Safe space was created for those stories to emerge without judgment or rancor. Not all have to agree. All perspectives are shared and received.

Dani did note that those who are more theologically conservative tend not to choose them as their means of having their spiritual needs met. They are intentional about teaching that conservative perspectives are not evil. The also teach that the "rant mode" is not productive.

ReImagine is not affiliated with any denominational body. They do consult with a lot of churches, many of which are connected to a denomination. They provide mentoring to many ordained clergy. They move within, and around, a wide variety of groups and affiliated bodies. They see themselves as a part of the larger church. This statement was profoundly moving to me—and I will confess that a part of my purpose in writing this book is to help the larger church see them as an integral, valued, and contributing part of the Body of Christ.

Dani herself for a time wanted nothing to do with church. She carried her own wounds with her as a result of her earlier experience. Now that she has done some healing, she sees this very differently. She has a heart for Jesus and his teachings. She sees herself as a partner with Jesus. She does not see the church as wrong, but as in a state of evolution. She sees herself as part of a movement that is helping the church to evolve. She can be, and is, a part of that. She is one called to re-imagine Church.

She knows many for whom the need to differentiate themselves from the Church is necessary in order to heal from a past wound. She believes that the maturity of the Church will come as these wounds are attended to with care and compassion. People want to see themselves as part of something bigger, as part of a community.

Although not ordained, Dani meets with a circle of female clergy. Some of the people who are a part of one of the tribes still attend a regular church. What they share is their commitment to a group of people. They gather to clean the neighborhood park and see that as shared mission. They see this as the work of justice, of building community. It is not a ReImagine event, or a mission event: it is a community event. It is deeply incarnational for them—which brings us right back to where my conversation with her started, the exploration of making Jesus manifest in our daily living. Their call is to embody Jesus, and to do that by creating community. In her words, "we are present in the context in which we are."

Birthed out of Mark's creation of house churches in 2006 and 2007, this somewhat more formal structure called ReImagine evolved. They envision a Center for Whole Life and/or a Center for Integral Christian Practice coming somewhere in the future. They know that what they do is about transformation, of both people and of communities. They know that what they do is informed by the life of Jesus.

It's hard to explain what they do, Dani said as I was leaving. It is not hard, however, to see Jesus made manifest in whatever it is they do.

CHAPTER NINE

The Mount

"There are many paths leading to the top of Mt. Fuji - but there is only one summit—love."

- Morihei Ueshiba

When I called Chad Whitehead to arrange to interview him, he recommended we meet at the Red Rock Brewery in Salt Lake City. I asked him how I would recognize him, and he said, "I'm a tall, thirty-something hipster." I laughed, said, "Perfect," and then hung up the phone realizing I had no idea what a hipster looked like. Tall, I could figure out. I assumed I could fake the rest.

I arrived a little early to our meeting. I was driving down from Boise, Idaho where I had spent the previous day watching a high school baseball tournament. The day before, I left a cabin outside of Ranier where I had spent a week with two bikes and a case or so of baked beans. I was glad to have gotten to the Brewery early and just relax before Chad arrived.

I was seated at an outdoor table looking across the Salt Lake Valley to the Mountains just east of the city when I saw a very tall, very slender, hipster walk across the parking lot. Without knowing anything at all about being hip – I knew when I saw him he defined the term. He was, in a word, cool.

He dressed in that way that cool people do. I can't describe it at all; I don't have whatever gene one has that affords them the opportunity to choose just the right clothes and assemble them on their frame in a way that makes people want to look just like that.

His hair lay perfectly above his handsome face. He exuded both confidence and affability. We made eye contact and his smile told me instantly he knew who I was. His arm extended to me, and we shared a firm and friendly handshake. The conversation that followed passed between us with the ease of two people who, without having ever met, felt like they shared something already that bound them together.

Chad leads a postmodern community of faith in Mormon dominated Salt Lake City called The Mount. He is, in some ways, a disciple of Mark Scandrete, founder of ReImagine in San Francisco.

He says this with a sense of pride borne of both an admiration of a mentor he would like to emulate, and an incredulity that the mentor is there to support and guide him. He was referred to Mark by a friend of a friend who, on a mission trip in which both were on a search for social justice, told him to, quite simply, "Find Mark."

Chad googled Mark, learning what he could about him, enough to know that this was an important leader in the emergent movement. He went out to San Francisco to meet with him and arranged for Mark to be a Spiritual Director on a retreat held for the members of The Mount.

The Mount was formed back in 2006. Unlike many postmodern communities, this one was birthed by and has it costs covered by an existing institutional church. Chad described himself at that time as a dispassionate, despondent youth pastor in Salt Lake City who casually began attending The Mount in 2008. Within a month, they had him roped in as a very part time volunteer coordinator.

As a new church start that was started by an existing church, The Mount is a different model for how emergent, postmodern communities can form. There are always questions with this model how much latitude the planted church has to break new ground, and to report using metrics that prove worth to the institutional church. What is remarkable about The Mount is that Chad truly believes that, even though he is funded in his ministry by the existing church, he does not feel any restrictions placed on him to build a postmodern community. In some ways, that makes this particular example of an emergent community so very interesting.

The Mount was the vision of a senior pastor who wanted to plant a church for a whole new demographic. They provide a full time staff person and also maintain their website for them.

Before he started serving The Mount, Chad arrived at the parent church, Mount Olympus Presbyterian in Salt Lake City to serve as youth minister. In that time, he grew a lot. He read what Jesus had to say, and he asked a lot of questions—some of them about mission, some about money and its uses and abuses, some about lifestyle choices. He began to question whether or not his own life sufficiently demonstrated an awareness of, and commitment to, what Jesus taught.

Too many voices in the mainstream church responded to these deep, honest, and abiding questions with a sense of dismissal or minimization. Many would tell Chad that we live in a different context, the circumstances are different for us, and the culture of Jesus' time influenced what Jesus said. There was no one to talk to about his questions regarding the use of money, about his concerns about the environment, or about politics. It was just expected that in Salt Lake City, you were a Republican. The radio playing in the church office had Rush Limbaugh cued up every day.

Chad's wife, though, began attending The Mount. It would be she who would get him to shift gears a bit and look for the sacred in a new place. For Chad, the difference was like night and day. He felt it was so refreshing to be engaged in his faith life where open discussions could take place. The Mount came as balm to this bitter and tired youth minister. He now serves as their spiritual leader.

When Chad talks about the worship practices of The Mount, he begins by saying "We're not very clever." What he means is that there is a raw simplicity to the shared worship life of the community. For about twenty minutes, there is what he describes as "young adult style worship." That's followed by an intermission. Then there is a time for a teaching moment—all within the sanctuary of Mount Olympus Presbyterian Church. At the time of my interview with him, Chad reported that they had just started doing communion. This introduced some new tension into the group. There were those who were there because they had walked away from the church, and this felt either unsafe to them or like too much of a reminder of what it was they left.

Chad notes that he feels, in these moments, that he is "an in-between guy." I find that to be a beautiful expression, if not a mission statement. It is clear that there are times when these communities feel conflicted about what stays and what goes. Every community I visited with has different ways of dealing with these matters: the Bible, baptism, communion, etc. To some, it feels like the old, stale, painful way of being Church they left behind; while to others, it is less about a call to abandon the old as it is a challenge to repurpose the old and infuse it with new meaning.

Chad finds real value in being connected to an existing congregation. He says there is strength in that connection. Having said that, he is quick to point out that he and his members see no value in identifying as Presbyterian. There have been mentors from the existing church who have had very meaningful relationships with some of the postmoderns that Chad leads—but the endgame will no longer include accruing members who identify with a denomination.

Chad points out that The Mount is not looking for any kind of independence right now. The Mount is exactly what the senior pastor envisioned it would be when it was birthed: serving a different demographic. The Mount is a bunch of young people. They want to engage in mission—but they don't have the will, desire, or capacity to tithe. The ongoing support for this emergent, postmodern community will, at least for the foreseeable future, come from a strong, healthy, and vital church 2.0.

For now, because they use the sanctuary of the existing congregation, the gathered sit in pews. It's a simple setting, nothing fancy: some wood, some stone. People begin walking in around 6 p.m. They grab some coffee. For a while, they started even later than that—but then those with children felt that they couldn't finish early enough to get home with the kids and complete their bedtime rituals. So they start their service earlier in the evening.

This, in itself, is a very postmodern reality. Many institutional churches still worship at the hour established when the farmers could get free after doing morning chores, getting breakfast, cleaning up, and getting to the church—namely, around 10 or 10:30. It would take something just short of an act of God to change that time. Postmodern communities live with a flexibility that allows them to talk about how needs can be met. Decisions are made but never established as normative. They are always negotiable.

The worship has a very still, almost contemplative feel to it. There is also time for interactive participation—one of the hallmarks of postmodern experience. Chad does do some preaching, usually after an intermission. The night ends with prayer together. There is a band that plays—but, as Chad said earlier, "None of that rock and roll shit." There are no members. There is no functioning concept of membership. They have not exactly figured out how to navigate that yet. There is no interest in identifying anyone as, or electing anyone to, the role of President. There is no mission statement. During the school year, there could be as many as eighty there. During the summer, closer to fifty.

The preaching Chad does is something he identifies as postmodern preaching. It is not "some white guy telling the world what will be." Other voices are always involved in the preaching process. Sometimes the entire group gets involved. He will often ask for volunteers to blog about the upcoming text during the week. He is often blown away by how articulate they are and can be.

Chad points out that this group is not just different. He says, "We are called to be different." That is a powerful distinction for him. It is an interesting articulation of a postmodern mandate. There is clearly something different going on here. That is not just an accident of circumstance. There is an intentionality to it that is seen as a legitimate response to the impulse of the Holy Spirit. There is a sense of call in this. "Recreate my church. Speak the gospel to a new time and a new people who hear with new ears and see with new eyes. The former things have passed away: do you not perceive it." As Chad says—"We own this. If you want something more traditional – go find it. You have options."

He points out that this is not just non-traditional Christianity; this is an intentional recreation intended to meet the needs of those whose search for the sacred and divine is not being met by the current model of the Church. There is imperative here borne of a desire to keep the gospel alive.

Chad's first words after reflecting on this were: "We don't know everything." Those are the words of a committed postmodern: we don't know everything. We are going to live out our calling, faithfully and passionately and unapologetically, but we don't know it all. We don't need to.

If Jesus is true, Chad asks, then how are we called to live? And why don't we? For this postmodern, these are the questions that have always been on the table. This new way of being the Church is an invitation to an authentic and shared exploration of what might be possible if we take those questions to heart.

The Mount is the coming together of a community deeply committed to learning who Jesus was and what that means for us this day. Conversations are the points along the way that get marked. Time is spent learning to be good listeners. This is a critical growing edge for all of them.

In addition to the Sunday evening gathering, the mid-week options vary. Chad teaches that modern people need to sit quietly. They schedule contemplative sits. They do hikes where they walk for twenty minutes, then sit. They hike some more, then they sit. These are baby steps, he says, but there is an audience building for this.

At the time of the interview, The Mount had just completed a Tuesday evening Bible Study. It was what Chad called a "hybrid traditional study" modified by Mark Scandrette's practice-based study. Every participant was invited to do something based on what they hear in the text, and then everyone returns to talk about their experience. For this study, they looked at Jonah and Ruth together. The theme, loosely, was "God's mercy for the non-chosen."

One participant noted that Ruth had to scrounge for food, and so she challenged herself to go do that. Someone else noted the theme in the narrative about playing favorites and decided to focus attention on prejudice. They organized an art show in which the theme of the art was to portray a time when you showed prejudice to another. Another participant wrote a poem about their resentment of Mormons. Someone else wrote a children's story about helping a young child with autism. They did that because they were working to overcome their own fear of those who are diagnosed as autistic. This combination of traditional studying the text combined with an action that follows, and then processing the experience of the action, is a type of learning that many are getting into. There have been, Chad notes, some who just outright reject this method, though, and who want to just sit around and talk about the text. When this group took over the gather, Chad tells, only five people kept coming. They would sit for two hours and talk. Everyone else stopped seeing the value in it.

When Mark Scandrette released a new book on simplicity, The Mount invited him to come and lead a retreat for them. The purpose of the retreat will be not only to focus on simplicity as a modality for living the way of Jesus, but also to create a new vision of these practice-based groups. There is a buzz of excitement at The Mount about this possibility.

Although, at this point, there is not a single focus as a group on a collective mission, the individual participants commit in various ways to making a difference. There are some who volunteer to support an after school program. One member mentors Mormon women who have been sexually abused. One works at local refuge for abused women. Another works at the farmer's market, sorting garbage.

When I asked Chad what his metric was—how did he judge whether they were succeeding—he said pretty quickly, "It isn't members, and it isn't money." He said they just can't do that. The folk who come don't give anything, and he doesn't always ask. If it were about that, he says that, without a doubt, they would be shut down. The funding comes from the existing church, and they do it because they see young people and families showing up.

I asked if this was supposed to be a feeder church for the existing church that funds them. He said, originally, that was the plan. Now, though, he says that most are beginning to think this postmodern thing isn't a fad. It's here to stay.

When I asked if he had any allies in Salt Lake, he said he did, but that they don't agree with each other. There is an appreciation for what he is doing but also a deep lack of understanding about how he does it.

Chad says that if there is one thing that he would like people to know about The Mount, it would be that, "We are a safe place." There is no theology of division he can find in the teachings of Jesus.

That feels like a good place to stop: The Mount, a sacred community inhabiting someone else's sanctuary in the heart of Mormon-dominated Salt Lake City, providing safe space to all. They are the balm for the bitter and the tired.

CHAPTER TEN

The Emergent Desert

"In the desert, the only God is a well."

- Vera Nazarian

Joy Lynne Schroeder is a byproduct of the church at its worst. She grew up a devout, practicing Christian in a household of family members who loved Jesus. That faith sustained her well through her time of childhood. As she matured, however, the particular brand of Christianity that she practiced became harder and harder for her to endure. She would eventually realize that her mental health was being threatened and, after suffering a nervous break down over it, left the church with no intention of ever coming back.

The preachers she heard growing up brokered in fear and guilt. To be sure, they talked about the love of God and Jesus. They taught about the good life made eternal by the blood of the lamb. They talked about the miracle stories found in the gospels—and testified to God's power to change lives even today. Witnesses were willing to share their own personal stories about the impact Jesus made on their own lives. And while all of this made her happy as a child to know and love Jesus, there would come a time when the accompanying guilt, fear, and doubt would overwhelm whatever kindness, love, and compassion could be found.

That guilt would cause her enormous stress. It would eat at her. Beneath the palpable fear of damnation, beneath the guilt borne of an inability to lead the perfect life—surfaced emerging doubts and questions about the authenticity of such a gospel. Those questions would haunt her—but they would also trigger the guilt and the fear that would continue to eat away at her soul and spirit. In time, the stress and the guilt and the fear would break her. She would be left with no choice but to risk alienation from her family and her faith and leave the church. It was a painful decision for her but one she could not avoid making.

Whatever relief was supposed to have come from such a decision was mitigated for her by a second wave of guilt and fear. The tapes of judgment, condemnation, and damnation kept playing in her head. Having now firmly committed to walk away from Jesus and his church, having told herself that the faith of her childhood could not sustain her, and having wrestled with the demons of doubt—she once again found herself unable to escape the enormity and impact of the voices telling her that because she left, the inevitable outcome would be the loss of her eternal soul. A second breakdown occurred.

Time would help. The intensity of the psychological damage done to her by the incessant preaching of condemnation would abate. She would marry a kind, gentle man and become herself a devoted, compassionate mother.

Somewhere along the way, she would come to the realization that she was still a spiritual being, on a spiritual journey, and in need of spiritual sustenance. Returning to church was not an option for her. Like battle worn soldiers plagued by flashbacks to battles fought years earlier, suffering from post traumatic stress, Joy could not even think about entering a church building without some of those fears re-emerging.

She wasn't sure what that meant for her—just that the need for something spiritual would not leave her. She would risk telling her story to others, and discovered that she was not alone. Many had experienced the same thing—and also found themselves searching for something they couldn't even name.

And so it was that Joy would end up opening her heart and home to many whose spirits had been battered and abused by the church. Before too long, as many as forty people would gather, every Sunday, in her home. They would discover the emergent church movement and come to the realization that they were a part of it. She would begin consulting with, learning from, and seeking out other emergent pastors. It would slowly dawn on her that she was the spiritual leader of a cohort of gentle souls who wanted to experience something that enriched their spirits and fed them for their own journeys in faith. For some, it would even be less complicated than that. Atheists would find their way to her living room and join the cohort. It wasn't a faith journey for them—but a way to connect deeply with others in ways no one else was offering.

I first came to know Joy when she was invited to speak at and attend the annual clergy retreat in the Southwest Conference, which I am called to serve. The entire retreat was built around an exploration of emergent Christianity. It was my hope that we could create an environment where what is emerging could be seen not as a threat to our way of being church, but as an ally in the proclamation of good news and a partner in a shared mission to transform our communities in service to the common good.

I had never met Joy. I knew nothing about her or her cohort, Emergent Desert. She was referred to me by a mutual friend, a UCC pastor, in the greater Phoenix area.

I contacted her and asked her if she would come and lead worship for us. I would learn much later that the specific language that I was using, so comfortable to me, triggered a response of fear and anxiety for her. She doesn't lead or plan worship. She takes on the responsibility of creating experiences that have the potential to be sacred or spiritual or meaningful—but she doesn't lead worship.

Additional anxiety would be placed upon her both by re-entering the world of "church," and by placing herself as an untrained practitioner of spiritual disciplines in a room of "experts" in the field. Only because of her friendship with the UCC pastor, and his assurances that this would be safe space, did she agree to come and do this. At the time, I had no idea what a risk she was taking—and how much potential damage to her psyche I was risking by making the request. I would only learn that much later.

Joy did come to our retreat. It was early evening, shortly after the dinner hour. We were retreating at a beautiful center north of the Phoenix metro area. Surrounded by the desert and the mountains, the glass walls of the sanctuary made for a precious setting in which to encounter the divine. With Joy were her husband, and a musician who often came to their home to lead music for the cohort. As the evening light faded to darkness, we sat in a circle together, about 40 authorized clergy and three gentle souls utterly open to what the Spirit might unfold. In the middle of the circle was a small table, with a piece of colorful fabric draped over it. We would have called it an altar—maybe it was, but it had nothing on it that would have been familiar to us in the church. Childhood drawings, assorted kitschy knickknacks, toys, a book or two, Lego blocks, etc., were haphazardly strewn across the table and spilling out onto the floor.

Joy began with some words of explanation. She talked about her faith journey, openly sharing with these strangers that the church abused her soul and spirit; that the abuse led to nervous breakdowns; that she left the church never to come back; and that she could not fully escape the tug of the Spirit's calling to her.

She told us she had no education. She had no credentials. She had no training. She was not authorized by anyone. She had no idea how to plan worship. She confessed her fear to be in this room with us. She confessed as well that she felt like she owed it to us as experts in this field to get it right. She spent some time trying to learn what it is we do when we worship, drawing upon her past experiences in the church of her childhood. After much time stressing out over that and trying to come up with something she thought would satisfy us, she finally decided that wasn't what she was being asked to do.

Her invitation was to let us experience a truly emergent moment. The last thing she did was tell us that there was no planning involved. Shortly before she came to meet with us, she assembled the assorted items that were on the table. She told us this is what she does. She leads a busy life, and doesn't have time to spend preparing anything elaborate for her cohort's gathering. What we see is what we get.

With no call to worship, with no introit or prelude to signal that we had begun worship—without us even aware that any transition had taken place, we listened intently as she shifted our focus to the table. Already curious about the theme or the meaning or the metaphors she was using to convey deeper meaning, Joy simply asked us to look at the table. There was no deep meaning she attached to any of it. That's how *we* work in worship, but that is not the postmodern way. Everything was there only for what we needed it to be there for. WE would bring our own meaning to it.

After turning our attention to the table, she simply asked us to sit quietly until something inside us invited us to go to the table and explore its contents. With nothing more to direct or guide us than that—we found ourselves wandering to the table and eying the trinkets. Some of us held them in our hands, turned them over, examined them, touched them, caressed them. Without knowing why or how, we all realized we were imbuing these ordinary objects with sacred meaning—and they were searching something out in our hearts and souls and bodies to touch.

Music started playing. A soft voice accompanied the guitar, and familiar songs were playing in the background. No words were spoken. I have no earthly idea how long that went on. I didn't notice, and I didn't care. In ways that organized worship always hopes to do but doesn't always succeed, I felt the unmistakable presence of something sacred, holy, divine.

Eventually, we returned to our seats. Joy simply asked, "What spoke to you and what did it say?" I became aware of the voices around me speaking. I wasn't listening. I was hearing, but I wasn't at all able to focus on the words that were being spoken.

What I was doing was looking intently at a child's painting. It was mesmerizing. There was nothing remarkable about it. It was a typical childhood drawing with inexact figures, primitive shapes, dashes of bold color. I kept wondering if there was a theme to it I was missing (sound familiar—we were doing the same thing with the table.) Turns out, there wasn't, but that's how my mind wanted to work at first. Eventually, I gave in to the notion that this was nothing more than child's play.

Minutes went by—many of them, I am sure—and I still couldn't look away. It was speaking to me. No one else was, though their voices could be heard as background noise.

At some point, there was an open space in the noise around me. No one else was speaking. I felt intuitively this was my time to speak. I told them this painting spoke to me. I talked about the simple, beautiful notion that the canvas was an utter mess—the byproduct of a child who clearly felt that there were no restrictions binding her, no directions to be followed. Stars were on the ground, flowers in the air, fish on land. Skin tones of green and purple were evident. A mishmash of disconnected items otherwise completely unrelated were assembled in this child's mind—and on this canvas.

What held me spellbound, what spoke to me, was the realization that having spent an entire childhood with those who kept correcting me, directing me, and requiring me to "color inside the lines," and because of that having spent an entire life to this point trying to reach perfection and never capable at all of painting in this way, here I was face to face with a child whose heart was unbound and who could produce a meaningful work of art without restriction.

What if God related to us that way? What if the Church were reconstructed that way? Without knowing it, I was crying. I was moved literally to tears. I have spent untold hours, days, weeks, months, years both preparing good worship and sitting through services planned by other experts like me. Rarely have those services rendered such deep and utterly profound meaning.

I tell this story not to argue that one model is better than the other. I simply bear witness that whatever she did was authentic. I call it worship—she doesn't. But what she did produced for me a deeply spiritual experience. It was sacred, and my encounter with the divine was real and genuine.

The moment did end, and what followed was about an hour of questions and answers. I don't know how many questions were asked and answered, but I need to say two things about the Q&A.

First, I remember asking her about sacraments. Did she do communion and baptism? She said that communion feels too much like church to too many—so they are very, very careful with it and largely avoid it.

Baptism, though, was another story. She had never done one, and until shortly before that evening with us, had never been asked to do one. But just days ago, one of the couples who come to her home approached her and asked her to baptize her child. This was a lesbian couple, and they had come to feel very much at home in the cohort. The baptism was an important thing to them.

Joy had no idea what to do, but she felt a real obligation to honor the request. There is something remarkably genuine in Joy's sense of call here. That's my language—call—but Joy was already beginning to feel what every authorized pastor feels about their flock when called to serve a congregation. These were her people, and the Spirit had entrusted these gentle souls for her care. She confessed that while she had no idea what or how or where, she would soon baptize that child.

I was watching the room. There wasn't one "expert" in the room who felt the need to teach her anything, nor was there one among us who doubted that whatever she did to perform that baptism, it would be an authentic baptism.

It was months later before I met with Joy and asked her about that baptism. Her face lit up when she talked about it. They would schedule it on a Sunday afternoon. It would be held in a yoga studio that some of the members of the cohort frequented. Joy would bring a large bowl, set it on a table, and fill it with water. The couple asked if Joy would be offended if they brought a statue of the Buddha, because they also found some spiritual meaning in that. Joy did not object.

And so it was that on a Sunday afternoon, in a yoga studio, filled with people who loved this child and her parents and some of whom were practicing and avowed atheists, in front of a bowl, watched over by a seated Buddha—so it was that an untrained, unauthorized woman with no idea what she was doing held a baby in her arms, prayed over her, poured water on her head, and baptized her. Welcome to the postmodern church.

There are so many more stories to be told about this beloved community. I will add only one more. Once a month, they sit in a laundromat and hand out quarters to whoever comes in. If you are spending your Friday night in Phoenix doing laundry in a public space—you are probably an overworked mother barely making ends meet. This is this cohort's mission.

They collect quarters all month. Joy's husband is an avid microbrewer, and every year they sell tickets to a fund-raiser in which he sells samples of his product, bands play, children enjoy various games, etc. The money from that fund-raiser is used to help them hand out quarters on the Fridays they visit the laundromat.

If anyone is open to it or needs it, they listen. They don't evangelize. They don't preach. They don't proselytize or convert. They pay for laundry. They sit. They listen.

At one point, as a result of their Friday visits, Joy and her husband took a homeless man into their house. They gave him the spare bedroom, and he lived there until more suitable arrangements could be made. This is the Church. This is the body of Christ. This is what Jesus envisioned—and Buddha. And Mohammed. And Abraham. And God.

These are children of the creator seeking ways to experience something profoundly sacred, being fed and nurtured in a community that loves them where they are, and then doing what simple acts they can to make a difference in their world and in the lives of those who suffer unjustly.

CHAPTER ELEVEN

What, Then, Are We to Say about these Things?

"I dwell in possibility."

"Not knowing when the dawn will come, I open every door."

- Emily Dickinson

I'd like to conclude this book with some thoughts intended to start conversations, not foreclose them.

Postmodernity isn't about your age but your orientation

As I travel around speaking about this phenomenon, I encounter people of all ages who resonate deeply with what it means to be postmodern. What I have learned is that we make a big mistake if we think this is about old people and young people.

When I spoke about this in one setting, a ninety-year-old woman held up her arms and shouted with some glee, "I am a postmodern!" She had spent the afternoon listening to me describe what it is that differentiates postmoderns from those who see the world through the eyes of modernity. It dawned on her that she had been living with postmodern sensibilities pretty much all her life.

At a presentation in Albuquerque, New Mexico, another wise elder listened to me prattle on about what was shifting with postmodern faith, and she said, "It sounds very much as if the Church is in a paradigm shift between Christianity as a belief and Christianity as a way of life."

She knew immediately what lay at the heart of the matter—that dogma and doctrine and belief, while important, weren't the same as living a life consistent with one's core values. She was proud to know this and believed that she herself was committed to participating fully in that paradigm shift.

The roots of postmodernity date back to the late nineteenth and early twentieth century, and began to take deeper root in the latter half of the twentieth century. It should come as no surprise to any of us that there are more than a few people living in their

143

later years who have been waiting for someone or something to give expression to what they have been experiencing most of their life.

In every church I visit, I meet people who say to me that they stay in their church because of the relationships they have built. They tell me that their church is very much like a family to them, and leaving it would mean ending relationships with people that matter. At the same time, they confess that they get very little from the experience that feeds their soul and spirit. These are postmoderns for whom institutional liturgies no longer inspire.

A friend of mine who serves as a middle judicatory officer in his denomination was meeting with his clergy. They were all complaining about how mundane their settings were, how resistant to change they were, how difficult it was for them to move the wheels of progress forward with any dispatch. After listening to them whine for a while, he interrupted the conversation and asked straight out: "How many of you, if not paid by the church you serve to do so, would attend your own worship service?" Not a single one of them agreed that they would. These are postmodern leaders who feel caught up in a static world, called to be a part of something that they see unfolding around them but not able or willing to break free from the ties that bind.

All of that is to say that if we see what is unfolding around us as a young versus old thing, we are missing something very significant. We are forgetting that the culture has been changing in this direction for two or three generations already, and that many of our own current spiritual partners are really asking for something that they are not aware exists. They cannot and will not be easily satisfied with the rituals and liturgies and disciplines that fed the institutional church well for almost 500 years.

Postmoderns are not our enemies, but our allies

I mentioned this in the introduction, and have repeated the refrain more than once in earlier chapters. I still want to name it here as one of the most important things we can say to ourselves.

The postmodern faith movement is not the cause of the institutional church's diminished capacity and relevance. That change was going to happen whether postmodern faith leaders figured out how to repackage the gospel or not. We dealt briefly in the first chapter with some of the causes of the decline we've seen in recent decades. The emergence of new ways of being in this postmodern world is not one of them.

The risk in thinking otherwise is that we repeat the centuries of political and religious unrest that plagued the western church at the dawning of the Reformation. An already established church saw what we now believe to be a genuine response to the impulse of the Holy Spirit—fully invested in the ongoing work of the Church to proclaim the gospel with integrity and authenticity—as a threat to its hierarchy, its power, its control, its orthodoxy, and its dogma.

Countless faithful were martyred, hung, imprisoned, tortured, burned at the stake, and executed by "Defenders of the Faith" who knew that such things were necessary in order to maintain the sanctity of their way of being.

The printing press did then what the Internet is doing today—accessing knowledge once held by a few and giving it to the many. It was as true then as it is today that some of that newly accessed knowledge called into question long held assumptions and teachings that built the foundations of the faith. Once this knowledge is held, the consumers of it have two choices: abandon the faith as archaic or recreate the faith in ways that respond with integrity to what the heart and mind cannot overlook merely for the sake of honoring past principle. As the great abolitionist poet James Russell Lowell once wrote in his landmark poem, "The Present Crisis," "Time makes ancient good uncouth. We must onwards still and upwards who would keep abreast of truth."

Postmodern faith is not the progenitor of the postmodern world. Postmodern faith observed the same way the Reformers did that too much has shifted that we can't ignore. Rather than abandon the faith to the dustbins of history, they actively create something that has the capacity to make it meaningful and relevant again. Long after present day spiritualists have lost their taste for scripture passages that we know are not divinely inspired (such as Judges 19), and long after the last chords of the pipe organs are featured as the means by which our hearts are stirred in worship; and long after trained experts with clearance, proper vetting, and full authorization are granted 60-90 minutes each week of our passive and undivided attention—the faith will be kept alive by those who have found a way to make the values of the gospel relevant without those things.

Because we both see the power of this gospel of love, of welcome, of grace, of inclusion, of extravagant welcome as a means to change lives and communities; and because we will both make use of the precious resources we have been given to care for and proclaim that gospel: we need to remind ourselves that our success is dependent on each other. Rather than two worlds colliding and believing that the existence of the one means the diminishment of the other, I believe it is possible that we all begin to see each other as allies. Rather than accepting that we are playing a zero sum game with limited resources, and that whatever one gets must be taken from the ledger of the other, I believe that we are called to recognize that we are fully entwined with each other: what one experiences as a success the other feels and benefits from as well. They will, after all, know we are Christians by our love.

If yours is a 2.0 church, be the best darn 2.0 church you can be

I was invited to be the keynote speaker at an annual banquet in a church located in an intentional retirement community—no one under the age of fifty-five can live there. They wanted me to come and speak about what is changing in the Church and the world.

When I finished talking about the changes, and what is happening because of postmodernity, we did a little Q and A with the church. The first question they asked was "How do we become this church?" I said, "You don't. And you shouldn't try. If you do, it will kill your church."

If you are a church 2.0, then do what you can to become a church version 2.1, 2.2 – heck, maybe even a 2.8 model. Don't be afraid of change. Accept it. Adapt as you are able and meet the needs of your worshiping members.

While I think it is possible for churches 2.0 to birth new 3.0 churches, I don't think it is possible or wise to ask one of them to abandon its familiar way of being in order to endure a paradigm shift. Adding a contemporary service, playing the guitar along with the organ, asking your pastor to remove her robe once in a while, using projections screens instead of bulletins, singing from a praise book instead of a hymnal are often difficult changes for institutional churches to make—but it isn't changing their entire way of being. Good leaders will always calculate what changes can be endured under what circumstances. I don't think any leader can or should ask a body that gathered under one set of presuppositions to change their entire way of being and abandon it for a whole new way of being.

Do I think that some of our churches are going to die? I do.

Do I think that those members who are left when the lights go out for the last time could have saved their church by becoming postmodern? I do not.

The simple truth is that, much as Catholicism did not die with the Reformation, neither will the institutional church die with postmodernity. It is likely to be the case that a smaller number of people will ask for that kind of worship. We will reach a point where we will try to save *every* church and invest only in those that the market share will bear at any given time. That's just good stewardship.

So, if you are a church 2.0 that believes you have a calling and a purpose and a mission and are not ready to die—then continue to be the best church 2.0 you can be.

You have postmoderns worshiping with you weekly

I often hear from worshipers and clergy alike that they keep attending their worship service because of the relationships they have built over the years. They can't quite fully express what it is about the shared worship life of the Church, but they know it isn't quite hitting their sweet spot.

These are mostly postmoderns. These are people who grew up in the church, or who have felt a spiritual hunger and who turned to the church to feed that hunger and, consequently, have built ties and relationships with people they love and don't want to leave. They are byproducts, though, of a postmodern world that doesn't fit easily into institutional structures.

Many of our churches have been trying to adapt to this reality. They struggle with whether to start another service, knowing that they risk making the sanctuary look emptier and fracturing relationships between people who are accustomed to worshiping together. They attempt to blend worship experiences, often leaving devotees of either style dissatisfied with the end product.

Arguments often ensue about how often to play the organ; whether or not electric guitars are suitable in sacred spaces or when they are used just how loud they can be turned up; whether or not the pastor should take the dignified approach and preach from the pulpit with a robe and stole, or whether she should wear jeans and sandals and move about while preaching; whether to keep the hymnal and the choir, or sing more contemporary music with a praise band.

If you find your church wrestling with these ongoing dynamics, then you, too, are a part of postmodernity's slow and steady creep into our churches. That's not a bad thing, but it will mean that churches have to think critically and carefully about adaptive changes that respond to current postmodern realities. Not all postmoderns are going to end up in postmodern faith communities: some will opt for one of our current churches, but only if some concessions are made. Finding the right balance between holding on to those things that matter and adapting new behaviors to meet the needs of the postmoderns among us has been, and will remain for some time, a very difficult challenge.

Discover your non-negotiables

I know I talked about this earlier in the book, but it is an important matter. I'd like to build on what I said earlier. Knowing the difference between what can change for the sake of the gospel and your mission, and what can't change for the sake of your identity is crucial.

I often do this exercise with churches. We spend time together trying to clarify non-negotiables. It certainly helps to know what your mission is. Knowing gives you a lens through which to filter questions about what is needed and what is expendable.

Is a building a non-negotiable? Can you be Church, with a clear mission in your community, without a building? I have worked with four churches in my Conference in the last couple years who had a building and then realized it was either an impediment to their mission or it had become their mission. Then they sold it. It was not a non-negotiable.

There are a wide variety of church possessions and practices that we hold very dear to our hearts and would find painful and difficult to let go. But part of preparing for adaptive change is knowing ahead of time what cannot be sacrificed for the sake of the mission and what can, and perhaps should, be sacrificed for the sake of the mission.

Knowing that something is a negotiable doesn't mean you get rid of it. It does mean that if and when consensus is reached that it now impedes the growth of the church or the fulfillment of the mission— you let it go, no matter how painful it is.

I submit that in this time of wild and crazy change, keeping an updated list of the non-negotiables is a smart practice.

What are those things that, when you lose them or stop doing them, you stop being what God called you to be? That's a tough test to ask of a product or a practice, and it's a high standard for something to try and live up to. Would you say that or your church's organ? Of your current hymnal? Of the color of the carpet? Of the pews? Of the stained glass windows? Of the governing structure your church has utilized for the last 50+ years? Of an Open and Affirming of Just Peace Church commitment? Of the annual garage sale?

How many of these are habits, and how many are essential to your mission and identity? The clarification helps churches know, in this sea of change we are living through, what is worth fighting for to the bitter end, and what is worth letting go of when needed.

If your church hasn't taken the time to list their non-negotiables, I would recommend you bring in a skilled facilitator and have that discussion. It is important that this process is done with transparency. These are corporate decisions, not unilateral ones.

Find out how it is you encounter the sacred

Worship is an honest and sincere exploration of practices that create the possibility of an encounter with the divine. I believe that at its best, worship creates space in which the gathered can seek the sacred, and having encountered that presence respond without fear or anxiety in whatever way seems most appropriate to them.

Postmoderns know this. For them, worship is not and will never be a series of rehearsed and or scripted rituals, language, or liturgies. Worship will never be assumed to be best executed in a dedicated building with elaborate architectural and decorative features that at one time were intended to, but don't always, inspire.

Worship itself is an overused piece of vocabulary that borrows the language of the institutional church but which has little meaning in postmodern faith communities. I now talk about encounters with the sacred or divine rather than structured worship.

The fluidity within postmodern communities when it comes to spiritual and sacred practices is a benchmark of their faith experience. They will meditate with Hindus, pray with Sikhs, sing with Christian praise bands, occupy back pews on quiet nights when Taize services are offered, walk labyrinths, pray the rosary, hang mezuzahs on their doorposts, place statues of the Buddha on their bookshelves, and read the Qur'an, the Bible, the Bhagavad Vita, and the Torah.

They like churches, mosques, and temples. They like rivers, mountains, and forests. They like candles, incense, and herbs.

They sing, they chant, they meditate. They practice yoga, Lenten abstinence, and Celtic spirituality. They know mysticism, Wicca, and Kabbalah. They use spiritual directors, shamans, priests, rabbis, imams, and coaches to feed their spiritual pathways.

If you are an institutional church that is part of a recognized denomination, it is going to be hard for you to change your stripes and meet all the needs of postmodern worshipers. But there are certainly some smart things you can think about doing.

One is to put every piece of your current liturgical life to a simple test: does this enhance or impede the presence of the divine? There is no way to answer that to everyone's satisfaction, obviously. What one worshiper uses to find the sacred may not work for the person sitting right next to them.

But this does suggest that those pieces in our shared worship life that are just there because they always have been, can go.

It also means that throughout a church's liturgical lifespan, all reasonable options can be explored. Those done with excellence, imagination, freshness, and authenticity stand a greater chance of speaking to the postmodern worshipers in your midst.

Creating partnerships with other faith leaders and communities will not enhance your own community's competency to function in a postmodern world. Those partnerships will have the added benefit of building networks that make for peace, lowering the risk of intolerant behavior that often accompanies simple ignorance of the other among us. Postmoderns understand that.

Each new exploration of a spiritual pathway will grow your church's ability to create moments in which the sacred and divine can be experienced. Those moments are precious. Every postmodern faith community knows that such moments are essential to shaping a life well-lived.

Have a clear mission, a reason for why you exist

Remember—not every church is going to die. Some are going to thrive. The ones that do will have a clear sense of mission.

Postmodern worshipers will sniff out institutions that have grown inward and that focus their time and attention on the maintenance and upkeep of only those things that pertain to the membership, staff, and property. Postmoderns will look for a faith community that exists as a presence in the community and the world. They will want to make sure that their place of worship shows an interest in knowing something meaningful about who they are and what gifts they bring to the table and can deploy those gifts wisely and effectively in service for the common good.

There is one simply test to determine whether your church is committed to its mission: read the agenda at your next council meeting. What percentage of the agenda items tests the church's commitment to its core mission? How much time is spent deliberating about whether or not the structure, the building, the staff, and the members are engaged fully in the effort to fulfill that mission? Is the stated mission of the church prominently featured in the minutes? It is a small, diagnostic test—not an easy, quick fix. Don't just type in the words of your mission statement on the next agenda and think: "Ok, we fixed that." This is a sort of "where your treasure is, there also will your heart be" kind of thing. If your treasure is your mission, the heart of your church will know it and every thing that emanates from the leadership of the church will reflect that.

Does your church have and know its purpose, its reason for being? A clear and strong and vital sense of mission that derives from and reinforces the passion of its members is an essential ingredient in vitality that trumps membership numbers and offering plate totals. Those won't save churches that are dying. The Holy Spirit will remain invested in those churches which serve a vital part of community life, and whose disappearance would compromise the ongoing presence of the gospel—the good news—in that community.

I have come to learn that finding a mission that drives your collective passions, and that every member is fully invested in—is the smartest and most potent thing a church can invest its time and resources in. Don't do it as a mechanism for driving new, postmodern worshipers to you or to save your church: those may or may not be some nice side benefits. Do it because this is what churches were birthed for in the first place—and without a clear mission you have lost your reason for being.

Bylaws matter; gatekeeping kills

I used to think that anyone who cared about bylaws was a polity geek. I went a long time in my ministry without paying much attention to them. I would read them—because in a very mechanical way there were things I needed to know in order to function well. Most of what I needed to know was smart things not to do if I wanted to navigate effectively the system I was working in.

I have changed my mind on that. I now see that the bylaws are an incredibly important document in the life of the Church. Good bylaws make mission and vitality possible. Bad bylaws impede health, vitality, creativity, adaptive change, and mission. If your bylaws are more than twenty years old, chances are they are impeding your vitality.

Most of our bylaws were written with an understanding that elected leaders are managers of the business, with a clear bias— once elected—the honoring the traditions, practices, and protocols established by previous boards and governing bodies.

This model was built on the assumption that institutional leadership will come to power in order to protect and preserve institutional identity. The more outside the box you are as a thinker, the more marginalized you will be within the system that creates power and maintains stability.

Most of our bylaws have a flow chart of power, whether we realize it or not. A council, or consistory, or governing board with some similar title, serves at the head of a web that could then include a variety of committees, boards, task forces, or subcommittees. The bylaws spell out clearly which task force or subcommittee reports to whom, with every line eventually leading directly to the council.

The council is the gatekeeper. Nothing happens that doesn't get reported to the council, which has the ultimate authority to either veto or affirm decisions made at other levels. If the deacon board wants to purchase new altar covers, then once they make the decision to do so they must clear it with the council—unless the council has already approved a policy that reads something like this: "When using the Miller Trust Fund, the Deacons may not purchase anything over $5,000 without Council approval. Anything under $5,000 can be approved from the Miller Trust Fund, a fund designated for the needs of the worship life of the church. Anything not already in the budget that would require money from the church's current fund balance requires Council approval." You get the idea.

Bylaws can be written with a different paradigm in mind. Rather than beginning with the notion that stasis and stability are to be maintained at all costs, shift the understanding of the leader's core purpose on behalf to the church to discovering who will be called to participate in the mission of the church, and in so doing help the church advance its vision.

The emphasis here is on trust rather than suspicion, on permission-giving rather than gate-keeping. Filtering every good idea through layers of bureaucratic structure over months of meetings kills passion, vision, vitality, creativity, and initiative. I would teach my leaders to ask two questions when someone came forward with a calling and a passion to try something new:

How are you going to fund it?
Does it compromise our mission?

My recommendation: Don't amend your bylaws; don't completely rebuild the structure. Start over. Find a church or four that has done this, use their document as a template, and go for it. When the Southwest Conference did this, the Moderator of the Conference asked our annual meeting delegates to trust them. He actually asked for a vote to suspend our current bylaws for one year, telling them that the conference council would act in their best interests even without functioning bylaws—and that in one year we would bring them a whole new structure to vote in. With almost no opposition, the delegates gave them the trust they asked for.

When the new bylaws passed a year later, created with a much stronger emphasis on trust, flexibility, mobility, innovation, and permission-giving—the pace with which things began to happen in the Conference was unlike anything we had experience before. Three items that had been on our agenda for over a year—one of which had been discussed for three years—were acted upon in the very first meeting. We haven't looked back since.

Postmoderns aren't invested in taking the time to navigate the often-complex structures we have built. Those structures served the Institution well, giving it a stability that helped it maintain vitality through long, lean years.

We are seeing that the investment in structures that ensure stability is making the kind of change needed to meet current realities very difficult to achieve. Structures that make adaptability possible when and where organizations elect leaders who know the mission and the core values are not only possible, they are preferable.

Interdependence
We need each other. This has become a mantra I repeat over and over everywhere I go. In the United Church of Christ, we have grown

fond of saying "No matter who you are, or where you are on life's journey, you are welcome here." I love that.

Now, though, I'm as inclined to say, "No matter who you are, or where you are on life's journey, we have need of you." Another way I will say this, borrowing language from Paul's first letter to the Corinthians, chapter 12 v. 15: "no matter who you are, or where you are on life's journey, no one can say 'we have no need of you.'" The prevailing mythology in America is that we are all independent bodies. We are taught from a young age to provide for ourselves, to pull ourselves up by our own bootstraps. We are taught that we make or break it on our own. The strong, the valiant, the brave overcome great odds by relying on their guile, their wit, their strength, their creativity, their cunning. Hero figures are built to model fierce independence. The archetype here is the Lone Ranger—a metaphor for the hero who does it all on her own.

It is a lie—and a costly one, at that. None of us are—none of us can be—independent. At every stage of our development, and in every aspect of our life, we are reliant on others for our development and success. Shifting our emphasis from teaching reliance on others teaching the value of strong, trusting, and mutually beneficial relationships is critical. It is organic. It is biblical. It honors our most fundamental beliefs about a God who invests in relationship, builds covenant, and calls for community.

I have often said of my denomination, the UCC, that our insistence on the autonomy of the local church is hindering our vitality. As one church after another struggles though a time of diminished capacity, relevance, and missional impact they do so often without either the awareness or the assistance of partners who could make some difference.

Lone ranger pastors who perpetuate the notion that this is our battle to fight alone are helping to destroy the churches they love.

I believe we should be cultivating partnerships and relationships between churches and other organic bodies who share their vision, their mission, and their core values. This should be as natural to us as breathing. I encourage all of our churches to develop partnerships with other churches.

We have a variety of ways that we do this. Some of these are new. We have some pilot projects that we are looking at, with the hope of replicating them in other areas. They include:

Triads

This is a partnership of three churches who are either going through a renewal project or are new church starts. The three-way partnership brings together leaders from each church that meet quarterly (or something close to that). The meetings explore internal commitments to growth, naming them to the other partners so that new ideas can emerge in a more organic atmosphere, but also so that there are partners at the table to hold them accountable. The role of the partners is to hear the strategies of another, offer some support, note the commitments, and check in with them on the progress or commitment to that strategy the next time they meet. The triads are set with both geography and compatibility in mind.

Resource churches

These are our larger churches, in each geography, which are often surrounded by smaller churches with much fewer resources. Some of those smaller churches feel vulnerable and are on a spiral towards rapid decline. They are very uncertain about their future.

A resource church, living in a very interdependent reality, begins discussions with its neighbors about their most immediate needs and how some of their own resources can be utilized to strengthen the mission and ministry of the smaller church. We make it very clear that these discussions are not about merging churches. Each church will maintain its own mission and identity.

Some of the benefits to the smaller church might include mentoring by the pastoral staff of the larger church to lay licensed pastors on subjects like preaching, worship, or pastoral care. They might also bring youth together from the surrounding smaller churches to join together under the guidance of a youth minister from the larger church. The resource church might be the one that purchases Sunday School material for all of the surrounding churches, perhaps using it first and then distributing it to the smaller churches six months later. There are no limits to the kinds of mutual benefits that a resource church could provide when exploring how this interdependent living can unfold.

Legacy churches

Once a church discerns that it is going to close, usually after a couple years of prayerful consideration and consultation, there is open talk with the leaders about what death with dignity looks like.

Living out of both a sense of resurrection hope, a belief that death opens up the possibility of new life emerging on the other side, and of legacy, an honoring of the missional impulses of those who long ago birthed their own church in order to bring the gospel to their part of the world: we work with leaders to imagine what the closure of their church will do to bring new life, new mission, new vitality to another church. While the death of any congregation carries some pain, grief, and sense of disappointment to the remaining members, the promise of stewarding the remaining assets as resources for new growth also instills a sense of pride, of hope, and of meaning not only in the closure—but also attaching to the years of mission and ministry for which the church will be knows. The final liturgies of these legacy churches are often some of the most meaningful and powerful I attend.

Pastoral support groups

Almost organically, and now with more intentionality, groups of clergy are meeting with some regularity to draw upon each other for support, creativity, innovation, and accountability. No longer just the gripe sessions that clergy support groups have long been known for, these clergy are gathering with clear purpose and intention. They discover that they really do need each other. Often with written covenants that describe how their time will be spent and how often they commit to meeting, and often then with formulae that proscribe how the time will be spent, their time is never wasted. Geography is proving to be a non-issue with some of these partnerships since a variety of technologies provide easy access to pastors across great distances.

My conference of churches covers close to 300,000 square miles. We are what used to be described as a large geography, small membership conference. There was a time when support from larger conferences helped us add to our staff. That is no longer the case, and over the years, our judicatory staff has gone from 15 (1 Conference Minister working full-time, two 3/4 time support staff, 1 3/4 time communications director, 1 1/2 time youth director, and ten other part time staff hired for a variety of functions from Committee on Ministry consultant to Evangelism and Stewardship directors) to 3—one Conference Minister and two office support staff.

We have decided to use some of our reserves to bring on a coordinator to help manage these relationships. They are far too vital, and the amount of work needed to maintain them is more than I can take on—given my already vast array of responsibilities. Interdependence is too crucial an aspect of our health, our vitality, our growth, and our mission to be left untended. We are not just investing in the concept of Interdependence as a good idea, but with some of the precious remaining missional assets we have. We can't not do this.

Final Thoughts

Church 3.0 is coming, and none too soon. Church 2.0 is evolving, and none too soon.

Change is inevitable. You either change by default, with no intentionality or creativity or purpose, or you do so with a clear sense of passion for your mission and a willingness to do whatever it takes to remain healthy and vital for the sake of that mission.

In time, church 2.0 will find a strong, vital, and vibrant ally in church 3.0. For now, however, church 3.0 is trying to find its way in the world. They will find that way, and will emerge in the postmodern world equipped to express the gospel in language and form and substance familiar to postmodern ears. Much of what they do will seem strange to the institutional ears of the gospel practitioners that preceded them. Some of it will feel like heresy to them.

The Holy Spirit, though, already evident in this movement that will grow, cannot and will not be stopped. She won't be hindered by our discomfort with what is emerging. She won't be slowed down by our reluctance, inability, and unwillingness to become what she needs the church to become. She won't be tarried by boards, committees, and governing structures that wait months, if not years, to adapt. She won't be sullied by institutional leaders who refuse to see postmodern faith as anything but heretical, vapid, and insubstantial.

Church 2.0 won't disappear. There is, and will be for quite some time, a need for the gospel they preach and the mission they undertake.

I leave you with two questions:

Can you partner with the Holy Spirit in the birth of this new movement, and in doing so make good use of the missional assets you possess for the sake of a gospel about to be made relevant again by those who understand postmodernity?

Can you see postmodern faith leaders not as the heretics yours forebears were labeled to be when they did things like tack 95 theses to the doors at the Cathedral of Wittenberg, translate the Bible into the vernacular, ordain women, and authorize the laity to participate in the full life of the church—but instead as friends and allies in a common purpose and cause?

Much of ancient wisdom reminds us of the danger that lurks when we fail to see the sea of change time makes inevitable:

"Behold, I am about to do a new thing: do you not perceive it?" (Is. 43.19)

"Time makes ancient good uncouth. We must onwards still and upwards who would keep abreast of truth." (James Russell Lowell, in "The Present Crisis")

"There is yet and still more light and truth to break forth from God's Holy Word." (John Robinson, to parishioners boarding the Mayflower.)

"God is still speaking." (The much-loved refrain of today's United Church of Christ).

May it ever be so.

Made in the USA
San Bernardino, CA
12 November 2016